FOREIGN INVESTMENT IN SOCIALIST CUBA: PROFITS AND LABOR FORCE

LA INVERSIÓN EXTRANJERA EN CUBA SOCIALISTA: GANANCIAS Y FUERZA LABORAL

José Alvarez, Ph.D.

Professor Emeritus, University of Florida
Profesor Emérito, Universidad de la Florida

FOUNDATION FOR HUMAN RIGHTS IN CUBA

eRIGINAL Books

Published by - Publicado por Eriginal Books LLC
Miami, Florida
www.eriginalbooks.com
www.eriginalbooks.net

First edition / Primera edición: 2016

Funded by / Financiado por: Foundation for Human Rights in Cuba

ISBN-13: 978-1-61370-090-7

Printed in the United States

CONTENTS / INDICE

FOREIGN INVESTMENT IN SOCIALIST CUBA: PROFITS AND LABOR FORCE

LA INVERSIÓN EXTRANJERA EN CUBA SOCIALISTA: GANANCIAS Y FUERZA LABORAL

TABLES

EXECUTIVE SUMMARY
RESUMEN

Socialism means the abolition of exploitation of man by man.

Socialismo significa abolir la explotación del hombre por el hombre.

Fidel Castro, Speech of March 19, 1962

This Report updates the one titled "Foreign Investment in Socialist Cuba: Uncertain Real Profits for Foreign Capital and Continued Exploitation of the Labor Force." It was prepared by José Álvarez for the Foundation for Human Rights in Cuba and published on purpose May 1, 2014. On Labor Day, workers in most countries parade freely presenting their demands. It has not happened in Cuba in the last 57 years.

Este informe actualiza el titulado "La inversión extranjera en Cuba socialista: Ganancias reales inciertas para el capital extranjero y la continua explotación de la fuerza laboral". Fue preparado por José Álvarez por la Fundación para los Derechos Humanos en Cuba y publicado con toda intención el 1 de mayo de 2014. En el Día del Trabajo, los trabajadores de muchos países desfilan para exponer libremente sus demandas. No ha ocurrido en Cuba en los últimos 57 años.

The opening paragraph of the previous version of this Report states that Cuba is a model of totalitarianism, oppression, discrimination and exploitation. The exploitation of labor is done with the complicity of foreign capitalists investing on the island in search of a quick profit. Although that situation has not changed, several events in the past two years make it necessary to revisit the issue. They include the renewing of diplomatic relations with the United States that may be heralding the end of the economic embargo on Cuba, in addition to the enactment of several pieces of legislation in Cuba and the celebration of the 7th Congress of the Cuban Communist Party. Some of these events will have an impact on foreign direct investment (FDI) in Cuba.

FDI has had a tortuous evolution after Castro took power in 1959. Cuba conducted most of its foreign trade with the socialist countries, receiving large subsidies from the Soviet Union. It was not until 1982 that the legislation dealing with foreign investment was resurrected but was set aside until 1990, one year after the fall of the Berlin Wall. The desire to attract foreign capital –and how little is the Cuban Government willing to concede to get it—is reflected in the numerous pieces of legislation enacted since that time until now.

This analysis conducted herein adopts a holistic (integrated) approach of the legislative process taking place in the past two years. The reason is that investment and labor force are intertwined. Although most experts allege that the Cuban regime has given again "more of the same", the truth is that there have been some timid measures although the exploitation of labor continues. Comparing the former Law No. 77 of 1995 with the Decree-Law No. 313 of 2013(ZEDM) and with Law No. 118 of 2014 that represents the latest law of foreign investment one can eventually find some minor differences in all but one area: the exploitation of labor.

The system of one employer continues. In addition to CUBALSE and ACOREC, there are 10 more employment agencies available to foreign investors in the Mariel Zone. Their relationship with the State remains the same: it is a monopolistic decision-making concerning labor hiring, labor salaries, conflict resolution and other matters.

Foreign investors are attracted to Cuba because of an ample supply of qualified and complacent labor force that will perform peacefully and as best as they can in order to keep their jobs. Furthermore, there exists only one Union. All workers are grouped in the Cuba's Workers Central Union (CTC) that functions as an integral part of the Government and the Communist Party. Those with intention or actions aimed at establishing an independent syndicate are subject to prosecution and may end up in prison.

Another control mechanism is the Penal Code, changed in 2013 to adapt to new situations. The draconian legislation includes the permission in Article 87.1 to use psychiatric confinement to those who require such treatment. There exist numerous prisoners who were given electroshocks as a torture. Article 8.1 of the Law of Criminal Procedure gives permission to Municipal Courts to determine the degree of propensity to commit a criminal act of a citizen and act consequently. Cuba is the only country in the world that lists such "offence" (propensity to commit a criminal act) in its Penal Code. Following Cesare Lombroso's theory of deviance allows the Committees for the Defense of the Revolution (CDR) to send anybody to jail because they are "dangerous". Independent labor leaders and dissidents have been sent to jail under Article 8.1. As an example, William Reyes Mir, who belonged to an unofficial group in Banes, Holguin province, was arrested in September 2007 and sentenced to two years of forced labor for "dangerousness".

The new Labor Code also helps in taming the labor force for foreign investors. The new legislation maintains the importance of the "work record" (*expediente laboral*) and it is not strange because that folder contains the information related to the worker since the first job until retirement. It is a control mechanism of utmost importance for a totalitarian regime and one more tool for the foreign investor.

The legislation prohibiting Cubans residing on the island to invest has raised protests because of its discriminatory nature. One of the protestors is Silvio Rodriguez, a long-time supporter of the regime. His options are those called "*timbiriche*" that sells some type of food of dubious origin, fix flat tires or provide a similar service.

Of all aspects of the main laws and decrees, our purpose is to concentrate on estimating the magnitude of the exploitation of domestic employees by foreign investors under the leadership of the Cuban State. First, all laws and decree-laws clearly specify that for Cuban workers and foreigners residing permanently in Cuba there is only one employer; that foreign enterprises will pay the State employment agency in convertible currency, and the latter will pay the Cuban workers in national currency. If Karl Marx were searching for the most profitable example to illustrate his theory of surplus value, he would have selected the exploitation of Cuban workers by the socialist State in complicity with foreign capitalist firms.

The trick is twofold. First, the State allows the existence of three different currencies with arbitrary values; and second, the State collects with the highest-value currency and pay the Cuban worker with the currency of lesser value. Hence, the worker gets the trick and the State keeps all the treats. For example, with the exchange rate between the Cuban peso (CUP)/the Convertible Peso (CUC)/and the U.S. dollar being around 24CUP=1CUC=US$1 for any given CUC or dollar salary, the Cuban worker receives 1/25 or 4.16% of the amount the foreign firm paid the Cuban State for his/her salary. Thus the Cuban State retains (seizes) 95.84% of the salary. This is true for the foreign sector except for the Special Development Zone of Mariel that receives a special treatment.

The legislation for the Special Development Zone of Mariel (ZEDM) contains a timid concession. Although the mechanism of the trick remains the same, the allocation of money is slightly different. The Ministry of Finance and Prices set the personal tax rate for workers in the ZEDM at 5%. The ZEDM decided that workers would receive 80% of the payment negotiated between the operator and the Cuban hiring entity. The Ministry of Labor and Social Security sets the coefficient for adjusting the salary of Cuban workers at "10", meaning that the rate of exchange between the Cuban Peso (CUP) and the Convertible Cuban Peso (CUC) to determine the amount paid to workers would be 10:1.

It is obvious that all the preceding narration open the door to noncompliance of international treaties by the government of Cuba in complicity of foreign investors. They include, among many others, the Forced Labor Convention of 1930, the Abolition of Forced Labor Convention of 1957, the Association and Protection to Organize Convention of 1948, the Protection of Wages Convention of 1949, the Right to Organize and Collective Bargaining Convention of 1949, the Discrimination (Employment and Occupation) Convention of 1958, the Employment Policy Convention of 1964, the Universal Declaration of Human Rights, especially Article 23.

One question remains unanswered: How has this system of investment performed in the past and what are the expectations?

It is very difficult to arrive at a conclusion concerning how many firms and enterprises are already operating in Cuba. In addition to the lack of detail, there are contradictions between the

The United Nations Conference on Trade and Development (UNCTAD) estimates an accumulated foreign investment stock of just $215 million for the period 1990-2009 (including $97 million for 2007 to 2009). The figures reported by the World Bank are almost identical: $210 million for the period 1994 to 2009 (and $85 million in 2010). The International Monetary Fund's Coordinated Direct Investment Survey reports $583 million for Spain alone (end-2010).The North American Congress on Latin America (NACLA) challenges those figures in an article written by Richard Feinberg, because they "clash with the magnitude of foreign investment activities that are readily visible on the island and recorded in the annual reports of international firms engaged in Cuba." Feinberg then engages in a complex exercise with figures provided by an anonymous consultant with access to official data. He recognizes that the lack of information originates in the "Cuban government culture of secrecy."

Concerning opportunities, the latest *Cuba Investor Guide* and *Portfolio of Foreign Investment Opportunities* were made available. Foreign Trade Minister Rodrigo Malmierca announced that Cuba was seeking $8.2 billion in foreign investment for 326 projects. The latter figures include 80 more projects but a total value of $500 million less than in 2014. Forty of the 246 projects advertised last year are in "advanced negotiations" and have been removed from this year's portfolio.

Obviously, even with the lack of reliable data, Cuba could not reach its $8.2 billion goal last year. What about this year? The predicted outcome appears to shrink when compared to other countries in the Caribbean sub-region. The most recent edition of ECLA's report states that after falling to US$6.027 billion in 2014, the Dominican Republic (DR) and Trinidad and Tobago (T&T) are the largest recipients in the Caribbean, absorbing 37% and 23% of total inflows, respectively. At the other extreme, Cuba and Haiti receive only small amounts of FDI, despite their large populations. It is interesting to note that the DR and T&T received 60% of the US$6.027 billion, leaving US$2.41 billion for the rest of countries in the Caribbean sub-region.

Foreign investors looking for opportunities in Cuba should consider very it seriously since Cuba's past behavior seems to indicate that investing in Cuba not only could result in a serious financial setback for the foreign firms but could end with a jail sentence for the risk-taker entrepreneur, as shown in the text.

With the possibility of investing in Cuba after the embargo is lifted, a forgotten issue has been brought to light again. Its name is "Cuban Claims Program" and relates to the properties of U.S. citizens expropriated by the Castro regime in the early years of the revolution. A current list contains close to 7,000 claims. Not long after that, the Internal Revenue Service authorized those people to use what is called "The Cuba Loss" and deduct a portion of their loss from their federal income taxes. The arguments among federal agencies on how to deal with that problem have already started. Whatever decision the Federal Government takes, it will affect all concerned parties, especially if a person purchased a property that belongs to one of the claimants.

Our last thought relates to Fidel Castro's brief intervention during the celebration of the 7th Congress of Cuba's Communist Party in April of 2016. Although the system has yet to change, the era of his absolute power is over. He announced his upcoming 90th birthday and the likelihood of his near departure. He will leave behind a chaotic country, the product of his disastrous social and economic policies. The temptation is too strong: "*Adios, comandante*!"

Introduction

Socialism means the abolition of exploitation of man by man.

Fidel Castro, Speech of March 19, 1962

As in most cases, Fidel Castro was not telling the truth. Cuba's socialist State is a text example of totalitarianism, oppression, discrimination and exploitation. As an ironic paradox, the Cuban regime exercises its absolute power over the working class with the complicity of foreign capitalists investing with the Cuban government on the island in search of a quick profit.

The opening paragraph of the original version of this paper, dated May 1, 2014, remains true today. However, some events that have taken place during the past two years make it necessary to revisit the issue in order to update the situation in Cuba. Some events include:

- On December 17, 2014, President Obama and President Castro simultaneously announced a new course in relations between the United States and Cuba. Several policy changes were implemented in the following months:
    - the U.S. Secretary of State removed Cuba from the list of countries sponsoring terrorism; delegations from both countries held a conference on human rights issues; the two embassies were officially opened; a bilateral commission was established to advance the process of normalization; several joint meetings were held to solve problems in different areas; and the first commercial flight carrying correspondence to Cuba took place.
- On September 29, 2015, Resolution 20/2015 of the Ministry of Labor and Social Security was published in Cuba's Official Gazette No. 40, containing the rules governing the hiring of domestic workers by foreign companies operating in Cuba.[1]
- On March 22-24, 2016, President Obama made an historical visit to Cuba delivering an impressive speech that was heard by the Cuban people.
- On April 17-19, 2016, Cuba held the 7th Congress of its Communist Party. Foreign Minister Bruno Rodríguez launched a severe attack on President Obama's visit to the island,

---

[1] The full text of the Resolution is available in Spanish in the Official Gazette found in www.gacetaoficial.cu/

describing it as a "deep attack on our ideas, our history, our culture, and our symbols".[2] Contrary to expectations of a younger leadership, President Raúl Castro and the other members of the "historic" old guard remained in power.

Directly or indirectly, these events could have an impact on the future development of foreign investments with the Cuban government on the island. Of special importance is the potential complete lifting of the U.S. economic embargo on Cuba that would expand the investment opportunities with the Cuban State and contribute to the Cuban government's treasury with no direct benefit to the Cuban people.

The purpose of this update is to investigate what has happened in the area of foreign investment since our report published on May 1, 2014 and also consider some thoughts on the potential impact the economic ties with the United States are likely to have on the type and amount of U.S. investments on the island.

---

[2] https://dwkcommentaries.com/2016/04/20/conclusion-of-seventh-congress-of-communist-party-of-cuba/

Evolution of Cuba's Foreign Investment Legislation

The pressures exerted against foreign businessmen who want to invest in Cuba are terrible, they are unbelievable… they are very strong, because they want to derail at all costs the economic effort of the country, as part of its comprehensive plan to destroy the Revolution.

Fidel Castro, discurso de Agosto 5, 1994

After Fidel Castro took power in 1959, foreign investment became practically inexistent in Cuba. In the eyes of the Cuban regime it was not necessary since Cuba had plenty of resources inherited from the past regimes before becoming a special member of the Council for Mutual Economic Assistance (COMECON) from 1972 until its dissolution in 1991.

However, Law-Decree No. 50 of February 15 of 1982, resurrected foreign investment by regulating economic associations between Cuban government and foreign enterprises. Due to some inherent problems related to mistrust, the first association did not materialize until 1990, one year after the fall of the Berlin Wall. The impact of the disappearance of its main trading partners proved disastrous for the Cuban economy.

The desire to attract foreign capital was reflected in the new Constitution of 1992, whose article 23 recognized the property of mixed enterprises and economic associations. On April 21 of 1994, the Ministry for Foreign Investment and Economic Collaboration (MINVEC) was established to promote and regulate those activities.

On September 5, 1995, Cuba's National Assembly promulgated a new Foreign Investment Law No. 77 that granted more security to foreign nationals willing to invest on the island. After an initial flow of capital, the next twenty years witnessed a dramatic net decrease in the number of established companies. It became obvious that the 1995 legislation was doing little in helping to alleviate the country's dismal economic situation.

Under President Raúl Castro, Cuba's National Assembly enacted Law No. 118 on April 16, 2014 intended to correct the disincentives present in past legislations. Our original paper investigated to what extent Law No. 118 was likely to fulfill its objective of attracting a flow of needed foreign capital to the island. It also dealt with the method of hiring domestic employees, who suffer a radical exploitation. That feature is still enforced today.

That aspect of the foreign investment legislation was reiterated with the publication in Cuba's Official Gazette No. 40 of September 29, 2015 of Resolution No. 20/2015 of the Ministry of Labor and Social Security, which contains regulations related to Cubans applying for work in certain types of foreign companies.

An Integrated Approach

The Cuban government should revise its foreign investment laws to eliminate reliance on state-controlled employment agencies and other impediments to labor activism… Foreign investors in Cuba should use their influence with the Cuban government to press for Cuban compliance with the international human rights and labor rights treaties that it is committed to uphold.

Human Rights Watch, *La maquinaria represiva de Cuba*[3]

The economic measures concerning foreign investment adopted by Raúl Castro's regime should not be considered in isolation.

This analysis adopts a holistic (integrated) approach of the legislative process that has taken place between 2013 and 2015, intended to contribute in the effort to take the country out of the worse economic situation of the 57 years the Cuban leadership has ruled the country.

One needs to comprehend both the legislation about the investment and the one related to the labor force, because they are intertwined. Table 1 lists those measures aimed at attracting foreign direct investments and providing them with a complacent labor force.

[3] https://www.hrw.org/reports/1999/cuba/index.htm#TopOfPage

Table 1. Integrated approach of the legislative process related to foreign investment and the issue of Cuban labor exploitation by foreign investors, selected measures, 2013-2015.

Date[a]	Legislative body	Legislative measure	Purpose or objective of legislation
Legislation concerning foreign investment			
September 23, 2013	Council of State	Decree-Law No. 313	Creates the Special Development Zone of Mariel (ZEDM)
September 23, 2013	Council of Ministers	Decree No. 316	Definitions and regulations related to the ZEDM
April 16, 2014	National Assembly of People's Power	Law No. 118	New Foreign Investment Law
Legislation intended to supply a disciplined labor force			
June 25, 2013	Council of State	Decree-Law No. 310	Changes parts of the penal code and criminal procedure
June 17, 2014	National Assembly of People's Power	Law No. 116	New Labor Code
June 17, 2014	Ministry of Labor and Social Security	Resolution No. 29	It approves the reports, forms and records that enterprises should keep as established in the Labor Code.
September 29, 2015	Ministry of Labor and Social Security	Resolution No. 20	Norms and procedures to pay domestic workers in foreign firms.

[a] Date of publication in Cuba's Official Gazette.

Cuba's Current Foreign Investment Legislation

Our 26th of July Movement has never called for nationalizing foreign investments… Nationalization can never be as rewarding as the right kind of private investment, domestic and foreign, aimed at diversifying our economy… Our revolution is as much a moral as a political one.[4]

Fidel Castro, *Look*, February 4, 1958

The four most important pieces of legislation concerning foreign investment include the Decree-Law No. 313 of September 23, 2013 creating the Special Development Zone of Mariel (ZDEM) and its complementary Decree No. 316 of the same date containing definitions and regulations related to the ZEDM; the Foreign Investment Law No. 118 of April 16, 2014, and Resolution No. 20 of the Ministry of Labor and Social Security enacted on September 29, 2015. The four are supported by changes made to the Penal Code in 2013, and a new long-awaited Labor Code in 2014, which helps in fulfilling the objective of providing a complacent labor force to foreign investors. Although a timid increase in flexibility has been included in the new legislation, the listing in Table 2 still contains the previous concessions concerning capital and a slight change for some workers although the State shows a total disregard for the needs of domestic workers. In plain language, the Cuban regime has given again "more of the same."

---

[4] Interview of Andrew St. George with Fidel Castro in Sierra Maestra (See text in http://www.latinamericanstudies.org/cuban-rebels/2-4-58.htm

Table 2. Comparing selected features of Law No. 77 of 1995, Decree-Law No. 313 of 2013, and Law No. 118 of 2014.

Legislation		
Law No. 77 of 9/5/1995 (Previous Foreign Investment Law)	Decree-Law No. 313 of 9/23/2013 (Special Development Zone – Mariel)	Law No. 118 of 4/16/2014 (New Foreign Investment Law)
Place of process initiation		
Ministry for Foreign Investment and Economic Collaboration (MINVEC) (Art. 23.1)	Office of the Mariel Development Special Zone (Art. 6, Art. 9)	Council of Ministers, after consulting with the Ministry of Foreign Trade and Foreign Investment (Art. 11)
Final approval		
Executive Committee of the Council of Ministers (Art. 23.5)	Council of Ministers (Art. 11)	Depending on investment: -the Council of State -the Council of Ministers -the State central unit authorized (Art. 21.1-4)
Types of investments		
- Joint ventures - Firms with only foreign capital - International economic association contract (Art. 12)	By national and foreigner investors as users or license-holder (Art. 17, 23)	No change (Art. 13.1)
Areas opened		
All except health care, education and armed forces (Art. 10)	Those related to the development of the zone (Art. 5)	No change from Law No. 77 (Art. 11.1)
Foreign investors		
Yes, in all forms	No change	No change
Cubans residing abroad		
Not mentioned	Yes, as foreigners, but not mentioned explicitly (Art. 23)	Yes, as foreigners but not mentioned explicitly (Art. 2.l)

Cubans residing on the island		
Not mentioned	Same as above (Art. 23)	Only in joint ventures or international economic associations (Art. 2.m)
Profit repatriation		
Yes, with no restrictions or payment, but only foreigners (Art. 8)	Not mentioned, but assumed to be the same as before	No change (Art. 9.1)
Fiscal obligations		
- 30% of net returns (Art. 39.a) - 50% in case of natural resource exploitation (Art. 39.b)	-Exempt in several cases (Art. 57) -12% capital gains tax -1% payment of tax on sales or services -14% of salaries for contribution to social security (Art. 58) (Council of Ministers' Decree No. 316)	- 15% of net returns (Art. 36.1) -50% in case of natural resource exploitation (Art. 36.4) - New several exemptions (Art. 36.2, 36.3, 36.4, 37.2, 38.2. 39) -Adds bonuses in specific cases (Art. 37.1, 38.1)
Acquisition of legal status		
After registration in the Cuban Chamber of Commerce (Art. 13.7)	After authorization by Council of Ministers or the General Director of the Zone (Art. 24)	After registration in the Commercial Register (Art. 14.6, 15.5, 16.2)
Protection against expropriation		
Except for public good or social interest (Art. 3)	Not mentioned explicitly	According to the Constitution, legislation in force, int. agreements and due compensation from mutual agreement (Art. 4.1)

Exploitation of Labor

In a socialist system there is no exploitation of man by man.

Fidel Castro, speech of March 19, 1962

Legislation after legislation, most matters related to the hiring, firing and compensation of the labor force have remained unchanged. Creating such economic dependence of citizens on the state is a crucial pillar of totalitarianism. Admitting collaboration with that communist premise shows that the intentions behind an economic opening to Cuba under the present circumstances are quite detached from the rhetoric that capitalism would bring about democracy and human rights. This section shows the extent to which domestic workers are exploited by the Cuban State with the complicity of foreign investors.

A System of One Employer

Cuba's government is the sole supplier of workers and the one that makes the decisions about contracting, wages and salaries, discipline, firing, vacations, social security and many others. With the closing of the State firm CUBALSE (*Cuba al Servicio del Extranjero*) in May 2009, it appears that the only State employment agencies available to foreign investors are ACOREC (*Agencia de Contratación a Representaciones Comerciales*; or Agency for the Hiring by Commercial Representatives), and AUSA (*Almacenes Universales, S.A.*, or Universal Warehouses, S.A.).

In the case of the Special Development Zone – Mariel (ZEDM), there are 12 employment agencies, namely: Agencia Almacenes Universales S.A., Grupo BioCubaFarma, Empresa Empleadora de la Construcción, Tecnosime, Empresa de Servicios de Ingeniería Eléctrica Cubana S.A. (Siecsa), Petroempleo, Cubatabaco, Empresa de Servicios Especializados de las Comunicaciones (Delta), Turempleo, Empresa Empleadora del Transporte (Agemport), Corporación Cubaron S.A., e Inversiones Gamma S.A.[5]

[5] Their website (http://www.zedmariel.com) contains the information about these agencies.

Monopolistic Decision-making

The Cuban state dictates the qualifications a domestic worker must have, and the steps he/she must follow, in order to apply for employment in a foreign firm. Table 3 shows some generalities in that area.

Table 3. Selected criteria concerning the hiring of domestic workers by foreign firms as stated in Law No. 77 of 2005, Decree-Law No. 313 of 2013, Law No. 118 of 2014, Decree No. 316 of 2013, and Resolution No. 20 of 2015.

Feature of Legislation				
Law No. 77 of 9/5/1995 (Old Foreign Investment Law)	Decree-Law No. 313 of 9/23/2013 (Special Development Zone – Mariel)	Law No. 118 of 4/16/2014 (New Foreign Investment Law)	Decree No. 316 of 9/23/2013 (Regulations related to ZEDM)	Resolution No. 20 of 9/29/2015 (Regulations by the Ministry of Labor and Social Security)
Labor hiring				
One state employment agency with most powers (Art. 33, 34)	No change (Art. 31, 32)	No change (Art. 30.1- 30.4)	No change (Art. 36)	No change (Art. 2b)
Labor salaries				
Paid in Cuban pesos; less than 2.5% of what foreign firm pays for them in US dollars to State employment agency	-The Ministry of Finance and Prices set the personal tax rate for ZEDM workers at 5%.[6] -Workers receive 80%	No change	See Column 2	Paid in Cuban pesos (Art. 22) Same regulations (Art. 8)

[6] Ministry of Finance and Prices, Resolution No. 139/2014, Official Gazette, May 7, 2014.

	of the payment.[7] -The coefficient for salary adjustment is 10:1.[8]			
Creation of an incentive fund for workers				
Yes (Art. 32)	Contributions are for the maintenance of the zone (Art. 44)	Yes (Art. 29.1)	Apparently not present.	Apparently not present.
Conflict resolution				
In People's Courts designated by the Government Council of Supreme Court (Art. 57, 58)	-Cuban Arbitrage Court of Int. Commerce (Art. 45) -General Office Director (Art. 46)	Depending on the case: -Economic chamber of Provincial People's Court (Art. 60.3, 60.4, 61)	The Director General of the Office and the Agency of the Central Administration or the competent entity (Art. 51)	The head of the State employment agency (Art. 16).

As shown in Table 3, the new foreign investment law keeps the monopolistic decision-making of the Cuban State present in previous legislations. Decree-Law No. 313 states that Cuban or foreign workers of the Mariel Zone must be permanent Cuban residents and must be hired by an employing entity designed to that effect by the Cuban State (Article 31). Article 32 specifies that the exceptions to the residency status and hiring are technical and administrative personnel with prior authorization of the proper Cuban authorities. The Council of Ministers' Decree No. 316 that complements the law regulates every aspect of the relationship between the foreign entity and the Cuban labor force. Article 35 specifies that Cuban or foreign permanent residents must establish a relationship with the State employing agency before being eligible for work.

---

[7] "Régimen de contratación en zona especial de Mariel beneficiará a trabajadores." *Cuba Debate*, April 14, 2014.

[8] "Régimen de contratación en Zona Especial de Mariel", "Cuba anuncia reglas salariales para empleados de la Zona Franca del Mariel" (*El Nuevo Herald*, May 10, 2014; and Ministry of Labor and Social Security's Resolución No. 14/2014, Oficial Gafete, May 7, 2014.

Providing a Complacent Labor Force

Shamefully, many foreign investors are attracted by the Cuban labor force they will have at their disposal. It is a peaceful, disciplined, "tamed," and educated group of workers where strikes are unheard of and who will perform as best as they can to keep their jobs. A trouble-free workplace is without doubts an important incentive to invest in Socialist Cuba.

Only one (State controlled) Union

The Cuban workers have no support from their alleged union representative for it is part of the State. The *Central de Trabajadores de Cuba* (CTC - Cuba's Workers Central Union), the only recognized syndicate is not a legitimate workers' organization; it is an appendage of the government and the Communist Party.[9] The reader is invited to look for an event showing CTC standing against the Cuban regime to defend one single worker. Furthermore, since the revolution took power in 1959, May 1st parades are demonstrations of workers' alleged unanimous support to the regime rather than an opportunity to present their demands. Not one in more than 57 years!

Ironically, Article 54 of the Constitution of 1976 (as amended in 1992)[10] guarantees to workers the rights of assembly, demonstration and association. The social and mass organizations have all the facilities they need to carry out those activities in which the members have full freedom of speech and opinion based on the unlimited right of initiative and criticism. Obviously, as in many other cases, the Cuban regime is violating its own law.

On October 21, 2013, the Cuban regime was seeking long prison terms against independent labor leaders Vladimir Morera and Jorge Ramírez Calderón, of the "Cuban Federation of Independent Workers," a non-state entity not recognized by the government. Although imprisoned since September 2012, the regime was asking for eight and five more years, respectively. The charges included disobedience, public disorder and contempt.[11] Both were freed because the mediation of the Catholic Church and departed for the United States on March 2016.[12]

---

[9] Efrén Córdova and Eduardo García Moure, *Modern slavery: Labor conditions in Cuba,* ICCAS Occasional Paper Series, University of Miami, April 2000 (http://www6.miami.edu/ iccas/ laborENG.pdf).

[10] http://www.constitutionnet.org/files/Cuba%20Constitution.pdf.

[11] http://www.capitolhillcubans.com/2013/10/cuban-labor-leaders-face-long-prison.html

[12] See http://www.diariodecuba.com/derechos-humanos/1458066317_20939.html.

A Modified Penal Legislation

On May 29, 2013, Cuba's Council of State enacted Decree-Law No. 310 that changes parts of the Penal Code and the Law of Criminal Procedure, published in the *Gaceta Oficial de la República de Cuba* on June 25, 2013. Its main purpose is to adapt the Code to the changing conditions due to the economic reforms that demand more emphasis in prevention and punishment of criminal activity. Article 87.1 allows the use of psychiatric confinement to those who require such treatment. Article 8.1 of the Law of Criminal Procedure maintains that municipal popular courts are allowed to determine the degree of propensity to commit a criminal act of a citizen and act consequently. Cuba is the only country in the world that lists such offence in its Penal Code. Cuba is also a country that uses psychiatric means for interrogating and torturing political prisoners, as documented by Brown and Lago.[13]

Interesting enough, Article 8.1 extends to the political activity the old theory of deviance advanced by the Italian Cesare Lombroso.[14] According to his theory of anthropological criminology, criminality is inherited and those "born criminal" could be identified by physical defects, which confirmed a criminal as savage or atavistic.[15] In the case of Cuba, those "born criminals" are identified by the Committees for the Defense of the Revolution or the repressive forces who do not need to elaborate on complex anthropological theories. Needless to add that independent labor union leaders and dissidents have been sent to jail under Article 8.1.[16] One of them was William Reyes Mir, who belonged to an unofficial political group in Banes, Holguin province. Reyes was arrested in September 2007 and sentenced to two years of forced labor for "dangerousness."[17]

A New Labor Code

The National Assembly approved a new Law of Labor Code on December 20, 2013 to replace the one enacted in 1984. However, it was not published in the Official Gazette until June 17, 2014. In general, the new Code is very similar to the old one. They share most of the restrictions. Like its antecessor, its main purpose is to maintain the workers on line. The restrictive and repressive measures against workers mentioned in other parts of this paper constitute hard proofs of the regime's violations of its own Labor Code.

---

[13] Brown, Charles J. and Armando M. Lago. 1991. *The politics of psychiatry in revolutionary Cuba.* New Brunswick: Transaction Books.

[14] Cesare Lombroso (1835-1909) was an Italian criminologist and physician.

[15] http://en.wikipedia.org/wiki/Cesare_Lombroso.

[16] See, for example, http://www.hrw.org/reports/1999/cuba/Cuba996-01.htm and http://www.refworld.org/docid/3ae6a85f0.html.

[17] https://www.hrw.org/report/2009/11/18/new-castro-same-cuba/political-prisoners-post-fidel-era.

The new legislation maintains the importance of the "work record" (*expediente laboral*) and it is not strange because that folder contains the information related to the worker since the first job until retirement. It is a control mechanism of utmost importance for a totalitarian regime.

The relevance of an integrated approach is again supported by Resolution No. 29 of the Ministry of Labor and Social Security (MTSS), published in the Official Gazette on June 17, 2014. This Resolution invokes the Labor Code as the legislation slowing the MTSS to enforce the records, forms and other information to keep by enterprises. The excessive number of documents has the prime objective to have at hand all the information (both for work and politics) for each worker in the country.[18]

A Flagrant Discrimination

Most Cubans on the island resent the reenactment of the scene that took place in 1977 and subsequent years when the Cuban regime, short of needed cash, rolled the red carpet to returning Cuban exiles bringing presents and cash for their families and friends. The new Law of Foreign Investment, as well as the one creating the Special Development Zone of Mariel, not only exploit Cuban workers with the complicity of foreign firms, but discriminate against them by not allowing the same privilege granted to their compatriots living abroad.

Complaints have surfaced since the very beginning.[19] *Nueva Trova* star Silvio Rodríguez, a long-time supporter of the regime, expressed frustration in his blog about the exclusion of Cuban residents from bigger- stakes business. And he asks the embarrassing question: "When will we, who stayed in Cuba to defend the Revolution, enjoy the same rights?"[20] I believe Mr. Rodríguez, deserves an answer: "Never, unless you try investing in a single venture of those called street "*timbiriches*" that sell some type of food of dubious origin, fix flat tires or provide a similar service." Needless to say, he will not need the money from family members abroad. The reason is simple: The regime he has been supporting for so many years do not allow wealthy Cubans. That is something reserved only for foreigners, selected government officials and their relatives and, of course, Cuban nationals living in freedom in foreign lands.

---

[18] The interested reader may take a look at the *Gaceta Oficial de la República* No. 29 of June 17, 2014, pp. 568-595. See http://www.cubadebate.cu/wp-content/uploads/2014/06/codigo-del-trabajo-de-la-republica-de-cuba.pdf.

[19] http://cartasdesdecuba.com/sube-la-temperatura/

[20] http://www.cubastandard.com/2014/04/01/cuban-emigres-may-get-green-light-for-investments/

Estimating the Magnitude of the Exploitation

They can say that Cuba is no longer a Republic but a hereditary monarchy and he, Batista, can appoint himself king. He can dismember the national territory and sell a province to a foreign country as Napoleon did with Louisiana... All these measures would be legal and you would have to incarcerate all those who opposed them, just as you now intend to do with me. I have put forth extreme examples to show how sad and humiliating our present situation is. To think that all these absolute powers are in the hands of men truly capable of selling our country along with all its citizens!

Fidel Castro, *History will absolve me* (1953)[21]

All laws and decree-laws clearly specify that for Cuban workers and foreigners residing permanently in Cuba there is only one employer; that foreign enterprises will pay the State employment agency in convertible currency, and the latter will pay the Cuban workers in national currency at a rate of exchange set arbitrarily, like 25 CUP = 1 CUC = US$1.

Under the Foreign Investment Law

If Karl Marx were searching for the most profitable example to illustrate his theory of surplus value, he would have selected the exploitation of Cuban workers by the socialist State in complicity with foreign capitalist firms.

The trick is twofold. First, the Government allows the existence of three different currencies with arbitrary values; and second, the Government collects with the highest-value currency and pays the worker with the currency of lesser value. Hence, the worker gets the trick and the State keeps all the treats. For example, with the exchange rate between the Cuban peso (CUP)/the Convertible Peso (CUC)/and the U.S. dollar being around 25CUP=1CUC=US$1 for any given CUC or dollar salary, the Cuban worker receives 1/25 or 4% of the amount the foreign firm paid the Cuban State for his/her salary. Thus the Cuban State retains (seizes) 96% of the salary. This method of payment is

[21] Castro's alleged self-defense during the trail for the attack on the Moncada barracks appears in numerous publications. The one selected can be found in https://www.marxists.org/history/cuba/archive/castro/1953/10/16.htm.

still being applied in the country, a different one was developed for the Special Development Zone of Mariel.

From numerous testimonies, I have selected one that would leave no doubts about the veracity of the former statement: the Government of Spain –one of the major participants. Sponsored by the Economic and Commercial Office of the Embassy of Spain in Cuba, Gregorio Dávila Díaz wrote an article entitled "Cuba's Labor Market for Foreign Firms".[22] The author explains that the salary is composed of three parts: the minimum wage approved by the Ministry of Labor and Social Security; an increase that reflects the professional status (qualifications and experience); and a coefficient of unknown methodology that is applied depending on the category (Table 4).

Table 4. Methodology and ad hoc procedures for estimating monthly wages and salaries for domestic workers of foreign firms in Cuba, 2014.

Employee Category	Worker's Minimum Monthly Salary		Coefficient[c]	US$ of Monthly Salary Received and Kept by the State	
	Cuban Peso (CUP)[a]	(US$ equivalent)[b]		Total Received by State Agency (US$)[d]	Share kept by State Emp. Agency (US$)[e]
Non-qualified	150	5.66	1,7797	266.96	261.30
Low-qualified	205	7.74	1,6755	343.48	335.74
Medium-qualified	260	9.81	1,6157	420.08	410.27
High-qualified	335	12.64	1,5658	524.54	511.90
Executives	410	15.47	1,5342	629.02	613.55
Directors	435	16.42	1,5261	663.85	647.44

[a] Amount paid in Cuban pesos by the State Employment Agency to the worker.

[b] At the rate of 26.5 Cuban Pesos per 1 US dollar. For example: 150/26.5 = US$ 5.66. (http:www.xe.com/currencyconverter/convert/?From=USD&To=CUP), last visited May 16, 2016.

[c] A coefficient of unknown methodology intended to fill the gaps due to levels of degrees and experience.

---

[22] http://www.icex.es/servicios/documentacion/documentoselaborados/icex/pdfs/cuba% 20mercado%20laboral.pdf.

[d] Amount paid in US dollars by the foreign firm to the State Employment Agency. For example: 150 x 1.7797 = US$ 266.96.

[e] The difference in US dollars between what the State Employment Agency receives from the foreign firm and the payment received by the worker. For example: US$ 266.96 – 5.66 = US$ 261.30.

At the exchange rate present at the time the original version of this paper was published, of 26.5 Cuban Pesos per 1 US dollar, a non-qualified employee would receive US$5.66/month (150/26.5), which is 2.12% (5.66/267) of what the enterprise paid for him/her at the salaries of the time. The percentage received by the workers increases slightly to a maximum of 2.47% (16.42/663.85) for Directors.

Although it is impossible to predict how many workers will be hired under the two new initiatives, the study by Dávila Díaz mentioned above uses 24,190 workers being employed by foreign firms at the time of his study. Although the State agency receives other income from additional charges, Table 5 quantifies the exploitation or workers at different levels of employment.

Table 5. Exploitation of workers at different levels of employment, 2014.

Level of employment[a]	Weighted monthly salaries per unit[b] (US$)	Income/year (US$)
1	398	4,777
25,000	9,952,525	119,430,300
30,000	11,913,030	143,316,360
35,000	13,933,535	167,202,420
40,000	15,924,040	191,088,480
45,000	17,914,545	217,974,540
50,000	19,905,050	238,860,600

[a] Number of domestic workers employed at a particular point in time.

[b] A unit is defined by the six employment categories. For simplicity purposes, the following distribution is assumed: Non-qualified: 30%; Low-qualified: 20%; Medium-qualified: 20%; High-qualified: 15%; Executives: 10%; and Directors: 5%. For example, in the first case, for 33Non-qualified workers the government receives US$261.29, but it is assumed that only 30% belong in that category (0.30 x 261.29 = 78.39), and so forth.

The calculations reveal a startling result. The State employment agency, by managing between 25,000 and 50,000 workers with the distribution of qualifications assumed, may obtain a net profit of between US$119 and US$239 million per year. The figure is rather conservative. After assuming that the average salary of a sales assistant was CP 382.01 monthly (identified in a salary table), two researchers[23] concluded that the State employment agency was receiving around US$256 million per year when all employees were considered. That figure was more than the annual flows of new foreign investments to Cuba during the period 1993-1998 (approximately US$225 million). Obviously, at least at that time, the Cuban regime reaped more benefits from the exploitation of workers than from the value of new foreign investments arriving in the island. There were no reasons to believe that the situation would change under the new Law. And it did not, as explained below.

Under the Special Development Zone of Mariel

Although still unable to retain their surplus value, the workers of the Special Development Zone of Mariel (ZEDM) work under a slightly different regime. Articles 31, 32, and 33 of the Third Section of the Decree-Law No. 313 creating the ZEDM explain the "Special Labor Regime" in that place. They repeat that all workers must be permanent residents of Cuba, and that they are hired through the State employment agency. Resolution No. 20/2015 covers the topic of the workers.

In the first half of May 2014 the Cuban government announced the definition of the parameters that would only apply to the ZEDM.[24] Although the mechanism of the trick remains the same, the allocation of money is slightly different:

> The Ministry of Finance and Prices set the personal tax rate for workers in the ZEDM at 5%.[25]
> The ZEDM decided that workers would receive 80% of the payment negotiated between the operator and the Cuban hiring entity.[26]
> The Ministry of Labor and Social Security sets the coefficient for adjusting the salary of Cuban workers at "10", meaning that the rate of exchange between the Cuban Peso (CUP) and the Convertible Cuban Peso (CUC) to determine the amount paid to workers would be 10:1,[27] rather than 24:1 applied in the rest of the country.

---

[23] M.F. Travieso-Díaz and Jorge F. Pérez-López. 2001."La inversión extranjera en Cuba: Pasado, presente y futuro." In M. Martín, M. García, F.J. Sáez (Eds.) *La actual economía cubana a debate – Homenaje a Julián Alienes Urosa.* Granada:Universidad, p. 149.

[24] "Queda definido impuesto para personal de Zona Especial Mariel", *Cuba Debate*, May 8, 2014.

[25] Ministry of Finance and Prices, Resolution No. 139/2014, Official Gazette, May 7, 2014.

[26] "Régimen de contratación en zona especial de Mariel beneficiará a trabajadores." *Cuba Debate*, April 14, 2014.

[27] "Régimen de contratación en Zona Especial de Mariel", "Cuba anuncia reglas salariales para empleados de la Zona Franca del Mariel" (*El Nuevo Herald*, May 10, 2014; and Ministry of Labor and Social Security's Resolution No. 14/2014, Official Gazette, May 7, 2014.

A Trifecta of Exploitation

Trifecta is defined as "a bet in which the person betting forecasts the first three finishers in a race in the correct order". In this case, the "correct" order in chronological order and, perhaps, in degree of exploitation, from more to less, would be: a worker in the state sector, a firm in the foreign investment sector; and the Special Development Zone of Mariel (ZEDM).

A hypothetical example shows how payments are calculated for the Cuban personnel working in the ZEDM. The agreement between the State employment agency and the foreign firm sets this salary at 1,000 CUP per month. Calculating the 80-20 split between the worker and the State employment agency, the worker would receive 800 CUP (1000 x 0.8) and the State employment agency 200 CUP (1000 x 0.2). The coefficient of 10 would increase his/her salary to 8,000 CUP per month (800 x 10). The personal tax (5%) on an income of 8,000 CUP would be 400 CUP, leaving a net salary of 7,600 CUP. The worker needs to convert those pesos to CUC (24 CUP: 1CUC, which is the current exchange rate). Therefore, he/she receives 317 CUC (7600 / 24) out of the amount paid by the foreign investor. The remaining 683 CUC goes to the State Employment Agency. In percentages, the worker receives 31.7% (317/1000) and the State keeps the remaining 68.3%.[28] (Table 6).

Table 6. Monthly salary comparison among two different classes of Cuban workers in a joint venture and in the ZEDM.

Joint Venture		ZEDM	
Share to worker	Share to State Employment Agency	Share to worker	Share to State Employment Agency
2.47%	97.53%	31.7%	68.3%

Most people are familiar with George Orwell's book *Animal farm.* The pigs that control the government in the novel issued a proclamation: "All animals are equal, but some animals are more equal than others." Although the saying is directed to the governing class, one can use it for our example of the exploitation of the working class by the Cuban State: "All employees are exploited, but some employees are more exploited than others." Table 7 has proved the statement to be correct and in contradiction with its Constitution, whose Article 9 declares: The State a) implements the

[28] The example appears in an article by Rene Tamayo titled "Definen impuesto sobre ingresos personales para trabajadores" in *Juventud Rebelde,* May 7, 2016 in http://www.juventudrebelde.cu/cuba/2014-05-07/definen-impuesto-sobre-ingresos-personales-para-trabajadores-contratados/

will of the working people and sustains the ideology and the norms of coexistence, and of conduct typical of the society free from exploitation of man by man." It also contradicts Article 41: "All citizens have equal rights and are subject to equal duties."

Noncompliance of Current International Agreements

I advocated for the cancellation of the least developed countries' external debt and for considerable debt relief for many others. I also spoke out for the removal of the International Monetary Fund. It is time that the Third World countries demand to be free from a mechanism that has not ensured the stability of the world economy. . . I said that another Nuremberg trial was needed to pass sentence on the genocide committed by the current world economic order.[29]

Fidel Castro, *Interview with Federico Mayor Zaragoza*, January 2000

Table 7. Noncompliance of International treaties and conventions in the area of labor.

Organization/ Treaty or Convention	Violation of the Mandate
CO29 – Forced Labor Convention, 1930 (No. 29), and C105 – Abolition of Forced Labor Convention, 1957 (No. 105). ILO C029 and C105.	Cuba has used forced and compulsory labor by sending workers to permanent agricultural camps as a means of political coercion and education and punishment for holding expressing opposing political views. In addition, labor mobilizations to work in specific agricultural development projects also violate these Conventions.
CO87 – Freedom of Association and Protection to Organize Convention, 1948 (No. 87)	Article 1g) of the new Labor Code grants the workers "the right to associate themselves voluntarily and establish Unions." In practice, it is not allowed.
CO95 – Protection of Wages Convention, 1949 (No. 05)	Cuba violates this Convention that prohibits deductions from wages with a view to insuring a direct or indirect payment for obtaining or retaining employment made to a state intermediary agency.
CO98 – Right to Organize and Collective Bargaining	Collective bargaining is nonexistent in Cuba.

[29]Fidel Castro: cancel Third World debt, end corporate tyranny, July 26, 2000 in https://www.greenleft.org.au/node/21854.

Convention, 1949 (No. 98)	
CO111 – Discrimination (Employment and Occupation) Convention, 1958 (No. 111)	By selecting the workers to supply to foreign enterprises, Cuba does not follow the mandate of equality of opportunity or treatment in employment and occupation.
CO122 – Employment Policy Convention, 1964 (No. 122)	Cuba's policy is of selecting who works where, regardless of skills or endowments, and transfers are not the result of the will of the worker.
The Universal Declaration of Human Rights (Article 23)	Nonexistent in Cuba are: the right to work; free choice of employment; just and favorable working conditions; protection against unemployment; the right to equal pay for equal work; just and favorable remuneration; and the right to form and join trade unions.

A democratic Cuba cannot ignore that a notorious and public felony has been committed, and that rewarding the investors by granting them an advantage in time and cost of the investment ("a foot in the door") would be sending the wrong signal to newcomers.[30]

At this point, it is necessary to mention that Spain, Canada, Italy, France, Venezuela and other countries that have appeared at the top of the list of countries with the largest number of joint ventures on the island, have enacted legislation to protect their workers from the illegal and repressive practices in their countries, including those of foreign investors.[31] Readers should be aware of the fact that many of the Cuban-Americans considering investing in Cuba who have become citizens of Spain, are now part of the European Union's policy towards the Cuban regime, doubling their legal and moral responsibility in this issue.

Cuban workers and the organizations representing them have raised their opposition to this state of affairs. Every year, the ILO receives complaints regarding the abuses that the Cuban regime exerts over Cuban workers.[32] Conferences –like those of the Working Group on Best Business Practices in Cuba—have been held to make the world opinion aware of these unfair practices.[33]

From Cuba, the clandestine documentary entitled *Bajo el cielo cubano* [Under Cuban skies][34], contains accusations made in 2010 by independent labor leaders in Cuba of the exploitation of Cuban workers in general and in hotels operated by foreign firms in particular. Independent labor

---

[30] Alberto Luzárraga, "Socialist Cuba – The nullity of the foreign investment contracts due to an illicit cause: to defraud the Cuban worker," ASCE 11 (2001): 250-257.

[31] See Spain's Penal Code at http://www.wipo.int/wipolex/en/details.jsp?id=1399; Canada's Labor Code at http://laws-lois.justice.gc.ca/eng/acts/L-2/. French labor law relating to doing business in France is at http://www.ssalt.org/pdfs/France/France_French_Labor_Law.pdf.

[32] See, for example, http://www.cubanet.org/sindical/docs/d06080101e.shtml; http://www.sigloxxi.org/Archivo/oit.htm; http://www.ilo.org/Search3/search.do;jsessionid=07BD26148B9AE52D5FDE5047DD48E958?searchWhat=denuncian+a+Cuba.

[33] http://pdf.usaid.gov/pdf_docs/PDABT912.pdf.

[34] The documentary can be seen at http://undercubanskies.com/Spanish/index.html.

organizations have been fighting to gain a space but its leaders end up in jail most of the times.[35] One question remains unanswered: How has this system of investments performed in the past and what are the expectations?

[35] http://freetradeunionism.org/archives/ituc-cites-cubas-2009-labor-union-violations/.

Funding Follies: Parasitism at its Best

This time is different: Eight centuries of financial folly, authored by Carmen M. Reinhart and Kenneth S. Rogoff,[36] portrays the world scenario of lending, borrowing, crashing –and recovering– through a maze of financial crisis. Each time, the experts have predicted that "this time is different". Yet the authors' analysis of 800 years presents enough evidence to deny the experts' soothsaying.

In the case of over 57 years, Castro's Cuba testifies to the fact that all those years have not been different. My book titled *Fidel Castro's agricultural follies: absurdity, waste and parasitism,*[37] proclaims that this time is NOT going to be different. Almost six decades of failures and defaults support that statement.

Fidel Castro did not invent any new management technique to finance hundreds of agricultural projects, which have already disappeared from the Cuban landscape. Since arriving in power in 1959, Castro has had free financing at his disposal:

- First source (1959-1960): misappropriated assets by Batista's dictatorship: over $25b.
- Second source (1959-1963): The land and its improvements: 25 million acres.
- Third source (1960): Urban housing: several billions of dollars.
- Fourth source (1960): Industrial and banking sectors: the Foreign Claims Settlement Commission listed $1.8b for U.S. citizens and $6.9 billion for Cuban exiles.
- Fifth source (1961): Currency holdings: of de 1,187 million pesos in circulation, 724 millions were surrendered, 424 were assumed out of the country, and 39 million were assumed to be in "counter-revolutionary" hands.
- Sixth source (1968): whatever was left, totaling 55,636 small businesses.
- Wear and tear, an important part of depreciation, started a long road of deterioration and buildings started crumbling due to old age and lack of repairs.
- Then the game began: borrow → default → forgive → borrow.
- The main target was the Soviet Union (1960 – 1990): $65 billion for the civil sector and $13.4 billion for the military (1960 – 1985).
- Western countries did not escape: $31.7 billion until 2008.

---

[36] Published in 2009 by Princeton University Press.

[37] Pubished in 2014 by CreateSpace.

- A long period of condoning the debt and start the cycle all over again has lasted until this day.[38]

No, this time is not going to be different. It is going to be the same.

[38] The process has been documented by Álvarez (2014, pp. 176-180) and by Daniel Munevar, "Cuba: What lies beneath the agreements on the debt with the Paris Club and other creditors?", Committee for the Abolition of Illegitimate Debts, January 7, 2016, in http://cadtm.org/Cuba-What-lies-beneath-the

Performance and Opportunities

Another measure aimed at this is a greater opening to foreign capital investment. Who would have thought Shafick[39] that we, so doctrinaire, we who fought foreign investment, would one day view foreign investment as an urgent need?

Fidel Castro, speech of 26 of July of 1993.[40]

Performance

It is very difficult to arrive at a conclusion concerning how many firms and enterprises are already operating in Cuba. In addition to the lack of detail, there are contradictions between the reports of international organizations and interested economists. Let us look at several sources.

The United Nations Conference on Trade and Development (UNCTAD) estimates an accumulated foreign investment stock of just $215 million for the period 1990-2009 (including $97 million for 2007 to 2009).[41] The figures reported by the World Bank are almost identical: $210 million for the period 1994 to 2009 (and $85 million in 2010).[42] The International Monetary Fund's Coordinated Direct Investment Survey reports $583 million for Spain alone (end-2010).[43]

The North American Congress on Latin America (NACLA) challenges those figures in an article written by Richard Feinberg, because they "clash with the magnitude of foreign investment activities that are readily visible on the island and recorded in the annual reports of international firms engaged in Cuba."[44] Feinberg then engages in a complex exercise with figures provided by an

---

39 Castro is referring to Schafik Handal, general secretary of the Communist Party of El Salvador, who was present in the ceremony.

40 http://www.cuba.cu/gobierno/discursos/1993/esp/f260793e.html.

41 UNCTAD, *World Investment Report, 2010,* as it appears in NACLA's report below.

42 World Development Indicators, the World Bank Database, data.worldbank.org/data-catalog/world-development-indicators.

43 Reporting Economy: Spain, *International Monetary Fund,* Table I-1: Inward Direct Positions, as of End-2011 (elibrary-data.imf.org)

44 "Foreign investment in the new Cuban economy," by Richard Feinberg. Published on NACLA (htpps://nacla.org).

anonymous consultant with access to official data. He recognizes that the lack of information originates in the "Cuban government culture of secrecy."

Opportunities

The 33rd edition of The Havana International Fair (FIHAV) took place on 2 to 8 November of 2015 at EXPOCUBA. As usual, its main objective was to bring together organizations from all over the world interested in doing business and investing in Cuba. The year 2015 had the special feature of a potential lifting of the U.S. embargo that would increase the presence of investors from that country in Cuba. The event attracted 4,500 exhibitors from more than 60 countries and around 150,000 delegates. FIHAV has consolidated itself as the main channel to promote Cuba's commercial links with the rest of the world.

Three important events took place during the ceremonies. The latest ***Cuba Investor Guide***[45] and ***Portfolio of Foreign Investment Opportunities***[46] were made available. The third important feature was the announcement made by Foreign Trade Minister Rodrigo Malmierca that Cuba was seeking $8.2 billion in foreign investment for 326 projects.[47] The latter figures include 80 more projects but a total value of $500 million less than in 2014. Forty of the 246 projects advertised last year are in "advanced negotiations" and have been removed from this year's portfolio.

Table 8. Investment opportunities proposed by the Cuban government.

Sector	Location		
	ZED Mariel	Rest of country	Total
Processed foods	5	32	37
Sugar industry		4	4
Wholesale commerce		1	1
Biotechnology (medicines)	13		13
Construction		6	6
Renewable energy	1	13	14
Industry	6	10	16
Mining		10	10
Oil		86	86
Transportation		3	3
Tourism		56	56
TOTAL	25	221	246

Source: Portfolio of Opportunities, Ministry of Foreign Trade and Foreign Investment, La Habana, 2015.

---

45 http://www.caribbean-council.org/wp-content/uploads/2014/11/Cuba-investor-guide-Nov-2014-Official.pdf.

46 http://www.caribbean-council.org/wp-content/uploads/2014/11/Cuba-foreign-investment-projects-Nov-2014-official.pdf

47 Jaime Hamre. "Cuba seeks $8.2 billion in foreign investment for 326 projects," November 3, 2015, available at http://www.reuters.com/article/cuba-trade-idUSLIN12Y3HK20151104.

As shown in Table 8, the new portfolio includes opportunities on healthcare, tourism, transportation, construction, agriculture and renewable energy. Minister Malmierca summarized Cuba's position in the following manner: "Under no circumstance, even without the embargo, do we want to go back to being dependent on one market."

According to minister Malmierca, the goal is to bring in at least $8.2 billion in foreign direct investment per year.[48] Can one make an estimate of performance with the poor figures provided by the Cuban regime?

Estimates of projects under foreign direct investment after the enactment of the new foreign investment law of 2014 are very difficult to know. Minister Malmierca states that 40 of the 246 projects advertised last year are in "advanced negotiations" and have been removed from this year's list. Of those, 6 are intended for the Special Development Zone of Mariel.[49] As customary, he did not provide figures. While most of those projects are joint ventures with the Cuban State, some were financed with 100 percent foreign capital.

Caribbean News Now publicized the approval of a Unilever Project valued at over $35m for a Cuba-Dutch joint venture that will produce hygiene products. This project expands the list of projects approved in ZEDM of Mariel to 11.

The Reality

Obviously, even with the lack of reliable data, Cuba could not reach its $2.5-billion a year goal last year. What about this year? The predicted outcome appears to shrink when compared to other countries in the Caribbean sub-region. The most recent edition of ECLA's report[50] states that after falling to US$6.027 billion in 2014, the Dominican Republic (DR) and Trinidad and Tobago (T&T) are the largest recipients in the Caribbean, absorbing 37% and 23% of total inflows, respectively. At the other extreme, Cuba and Haiti receive only small amounts of FDI, despite their large populations. It is interesting to note that the DR and T&T received 60% of the US$6.027 billion, leaving US$2.41 billion (about the goal Cuba is shooting for) for the rest of the countries in the Caribbean sub-region.

In addition to the arguments contained in this section, it would be very difficult for Cuba to reach its goal if the projections by *Cuba Standard* (CS) become a reality. The Cuba Standard Economic Trend Index (CSETI) suggests that from the fourth quarter of 2015 on through February 2016,

---

48 "Cuba seeks $8.2 billion in foreign investment for 326 projects", by Jaime Hamre, Reuters, November 3, 2015.

49 *Ibid.*

50 Economic Commission for Latin America and the Caribbean (ECLAC) on the basis of official figures and estimates as of 18 May 2015, p. 1. It can be found in http://repositorio.cepal.org/bitstream/handle/11362/38215/S1500534_en.pdf

balance of payments conditions for the Cuban economy got tighter. The Cuba Standard Business Confidence Index (CSBCI) indicates that the deterioration of perceptions and expectations for the Cuban economy continues. The score of 57.2 for the first quarter of 2016 is the lowest value since CS began measurements with this index. As to the intentions to invest in the Cuban economy, there is a significant drop. In the third quarter of 2015, 45.3% of business people indicated a rise in their intentions to invest in Cuba, while the percentage dropped to 28.8% in the first quarter of 2016.[51]

A recent Report[52] states that "Cuba and Haiti, which have to date received very small FDI inflows, would first have to attract those flows in order to perceive any significant positive impact." By the way, the same ECLA's Report states that Cuba "is the only economy in the region that does not report FDI data".[53]

Foreign Trade minister Rodrigo Malmierca has recognized that Cuba needs an annual investment of US$ 2,500 million US dollars to make its economy rebound.[54] He did not explain its feasibility or the procedure used to calculate that figure. Another Cuban economist did provide a more realistic scenario.

Juan Triana, former director of the University of Havana's Center for the Study of the Cuban Economy (CEEC), during a public debate sponsored by *Temas* magazine, stated the following: "Cuba needs to increase by almost 15% its rate of gross capital formation, its investment rate, to be able to later achieve an annual average gross rate of 4%. It will take 25 years for this country to double its Gross Internal Product (PIB). You don't need a scientist or a doctor to calculate that. I will die and my son will retire before that is achieved. To understand what we are talking about here, such high growth rates are neither an aspiration nor a goal or a luxury; it is this country's necessity, if not, we will continue postponing the wellbeing of present and future generations."[55]

---

[51] Vidal, Pavel and Johannes Werner. "Economic Trend Report. First Quarter 2016." The figures were taken from the executive summary of an announcement that appears on the internet.

[52] Foreign Direct Investment in Latin America and the Caribbean, ECLAC, United Nations, 2015.

[53] *Ibid.*, p. 72.

[54] The statement has appeared multiple times in the media. See, for example, Spain's *El Mundo* newspaper of March 30, 2014 at http://www.elmundo.es/america/2014/03/29/5336edd0268e3eab068b456e.html.

[55] *Ibid.*

A Closer Look at the Tempting Proposition

Earth provides enough to satisfy every man's needs,
but not every man's greed.

Mahatma Gandhi

At first sight, the investment projects appear to offer a profitable opportunity. A word of caution is necessary. Basic economic theory tells us that there is a trade-off between uncertainty and profit, which has been proved by numerous economic studies. Opportunity cost is also an important variable when considering uncertainty and profit. Not only there exists a relation between the opportunity cost, uncertainty and profits but there also exists a trade-off between them. Investing in Cuba conveys a high degree of uncertainty because of its risk.

Cuba's past behavior seems to indicate that investing in Cuba not only could result in a serious financial setback for the foreign firms but could end with a jail sentence for the risk-taker entrepreneur, as shown with the following examples.[56]

- In 1999, Cuba had 217 mixed enterprises from Venezuela, Spain, Canada and Italy.
- Between 1999 and 2001, 76 firms left the country and the number of foreign firms decreased to 141.
- In 2002, Cuba's government reiterated its commitment to socialism and central planning and more firms left. Those that remained on the island were victims of unfulfilled financial needs between 2008 and 2010. Tension developed between the governments of Spain and Cuba because of the impact on Spain's businesses.
- Lack of payments is a chronic habit in most of Cuba's transactions. Unavailable cash slows the process, resulting in complaints or closings.
- The likelihood of shifting investment priorities is always a threat, and the firms that are not included are pushed to the sides and practically ignored.

---

[56] Part of this information appears in the article "Empresas mixtas en Cuba: incógnitas y urgencias" by Emilio Morales, *Café Fuerte* (cafefuerte.com/cuba8477-empresas-mixtas-en-cuba-incognitas-y-urgencias/)

- At present, Cuba is undergoing a process of currency consolidation. The unknown plans create uncertainty. Firms with some degree of risk aversion should at least wait until the process is completed. (As of this date, June 2016 no known changes have been made.)

- Rampant corruption at all levels is not a healthy investing environment. Raúl Castro himself has referred on several occasions that it is the revolution's worst enemy.[57]

- Moody's Investors Service, the famous international financial firm that ranks the creditworthiness of borrowers by measuring expected investor loss in the event of default, downgraded the Cuban regime on April 23, 2014. Moody's based its decision to lower Cuba's credit rating on the increased risk of economic collapse of Venezuela, a key Cuban ally. It also considered potential domestic shocks from a disorderly political transition which translates into uncertainty about the future state of Cuba's economy.[58] However, on December 10, 2015 the same firm changed Cuba's outlook from stable to positive. The decision was based on several factors: a) Dependence on Venezuela has lessened since 2014; b) Continued reform momentum and increase rapprochement with the United States have supported favorable macroeconomic performance and raise the likelihood that the U.S. economic sanctions might be eased further.[59]

---

[57] See, for example, http://www.powerlineblog.com/archives/2013/07/raul-castro-asks-whats-wrong-with-you-cubans.php.

[58] https://www.moodys.com/research/Moodys-Downgrades-Cubas-Rating-to-Caa2-Outlook-Stable--PR_297308.

[59] For more information, see https://www.moodys.com/research/Moodys-changes-Cubas-outlook-to-positive-from-stable-Caa2-rating--PR_339779.

Testimonies of Former Investors

Nobody chastens from somebody else.

Old Spanish proverb

Since the government is involved in an anti-corruption campaign, foreign investors are likely to be offered opportunities that may land them in jail. All disputes are of the incumbency of the Cuban authorities. There is no possibility to take them to an international court of law. Here is a small sample:[60]

- We must start remembering the first case. He was known as Jordi, the first Basque investor in the famous discotheque of *Hotel Comodoro*. When the authorities called him to complain about the *discotheque* turning into a brothel, Jordi candidly replied: "good so far; the holy go to church and the whores to *discotecas*." It cost him $4 million and the expulsion of Cuba.[61]

- British entrepreneur Stephen Purvis spent 15 months in a Cuban prison.

- Canadian businessman Cy Tokmakjian was in jail since September 2011 without being charged until recently. At the end of April 2014, Peter King, an important member of the Canadian Parliament, based on the case of his constituent Cy Tokmakjian, alerted potential investors of the dangers of doing business with the Cuban regime. Mr. Tokmakjian is being blackmailed. The Cuban regime is requesting his assets to free him. Mr. King stated that "the international financial community should think twice about the blandishments made by Cuban ministers, diplomats and trade officials to make them invest."[62]

- Max Marambio, a Chilean who developed a business with Fidel Castro, fled the island when he was charged by the Cuban government. He accused the Cuban regime in a French court of law to recover his expropriated business but lost at the end of April 2015.

---

[60] The following stories were released by Reuters on 1 April 2014.

[61] Tomado de *Balance Cubano*, junio 11 de 2011 en http://balancecubano.blogspot.com/2011_06_05_archive.html

[62] See https://us-mg204.mail.yahoo.com/neo/launch?.partner=sbc&.rand=2qfmeuto269gb#mail; and http://www.huffingtonpost.ca/peter-kent/cuba-business_b_5228281.html. The latter has the suggestive title of "Cuba is open for business that might land you in jail."

- Sarkis Yacoubian, a Canadian businessman who built a firm selling automobiles and industrial equipment in Cuba, was arrested in 2011 and accused of spying. Mr. Yacoubian spent two years in jail before being convicted after a two-day trial for corruption and doing economic damage to the government. He was sentenced to nine years in prison and fined $7.5 million before being released in 2014 after having all his assets confiscated.[63]

- French entrepreneur Michel Villand established a chain of bakeries called "Pain de Paris", later expropriated by the Cuban government. In his book *My associate Fidel,* he denounces that his Cuban partners defrauded him by keeping two sets of books, then offered a ridiculous low sum for his stake.

- Cuba jailed executives of the British investment and trading firm Coral Capital Group Ltd on unspecified fraud charges. They were found guilty of minor charges last June and released for time served, more than a year later. Instead of deporting, the new law intends to find executives criminally liable.

- Stephen Purvis, a British businessman was detained in Cuba accused of a multitude of charges. He was liberated 15 months later.

- Cuba has closed more joint ventures than it has opened since the beginning of the economic reforms started in 2011. In 2013, the Anglo-Dutch consumer goods group "Unilever" ended a 15-year joint venture after failing to resolve a dispute with the government over who would have the controlling interest.

- Several diplomats who requested anonymity have revealed serious accusations: "The communist government sometimes lets investment proposals die on the shelf without explanations.... In the end, the entire law remains discretionary." "If a venture is successful, the government often wants a bigger stake. It welcomes foreign financing, but once a project is operational it wants to take charge." "Use the foreigners where it suits you. Spit them out as soon as their usefulness is over."

---

[63] Fieser, Ezra and Mike Dorning. "Where Obama sees opportunity in Cuba, U.S. companies see hurdles." March 18, 2016.
See http://www.bloomberg.com/politics/articles/2016-03-18/where-obama-sees-opportunity-in-cuba-u-s-companies-see-hurdles.

Two Considerations about the Future

The new Law of Foreign Investment reiterates the commitment of the Cuban regime to respect the property rights of investors. However, Article 27 of the Mariel Special Zone law makes clear the possibility of revoking the authorization for the following reasons: the lack of fulfillment of the essential obligations; for causes of public order or national security; reasons of social interest or public good; and any other reason is clearly stated in the authorization's resolution. The foreign investment law has similar clauses. Previous track records on that regard make it difficult to believe the promise of no expropriation. Furthermore, the reference to compensation is not clear enough and the law states that any conflict has to be solved under the tutelage of Cuban institutions.

One could only speculate about what will happen to these investments when the rule of law is finally established in Cuba. The judicial system will be overwhelmed with legal demands resulting from more than 57 years of arbitrary and abusive actions. The foreign firms that have conspired with the Cuban State to deprive workers of their rights might be on the defendants' seat. It would only be fair that the exploited workers receive their "day in Court" for what was robbed from them. Such claims will have a legal base because the countries investing in today's Cuba are signatories of the Conventions sponsored by the International Labor Organization and the United Nations.

A legal analysis by Alberto Luzarraga was published back in 2001.[64] In essence, the author argues that the structure of the documents signed by the investor and the Cuban State is such that "they are null and void from inception due to the fact that they are based on an illicit cause, namely: to make the Cuban workforce an object of commerce in bulk and to defraud the Cuban worker of most of his wages."

If Cuban-Americans, either as individual citizens or corporations, make the decision to invest, in addition to the potential legal problem they may face, they will be helping in the exploitation of their own people. The Cuban regime will not hesitate in stealing their hard-earned money in foreign lands, as it did with their properties at the beginning of the revolution for which compensation has yet to be paid.

---

[64] Luzarraga, *Ibid.*

The Sword of Damocles

What justification can the imperialists use to pretend to destroy this work of progress, of advancement? And not just progress and advancement, but of heroic progress under the imperialists' "sword of Damocles" of heroic advance against all his might, against all its resources.

Fidel Castro, speech of September 10, 1962

The possibility of investing in the non-state sector of Cuba's economy has increased after the renewal of diplomatic relations with the United States and the visit of President Obama to Cuba. But the Cuban Government actually blocks the private sector to benefit from investment or commerce with the USA now that is made feasible. Since actual investments will not be allowed until the embargo is lifted, many entrepreneurs are already developing business plans and looking for financing. Most of them do not know, or have already forgotten, what is called "Cuban claims settlement process." It relates to the expropriation worth millions of dollars by the Castro regime during the first four years of the revolution. Those traveling to the United States at that time registered their properties with the Cuban Claims Program of the Foreign Claim Settlement Commission of the United States.[65] A Current list contains close to 7,000 claims corresponding to an equal number of properties and a lesser numbers of owners.

The Office of the Legal Advisor of the U.S. Department of State has been soliciting advice from law firms with experience on this issue. There are several opinions. The U.S. government commissioned the Creighton University School of Law & Department of Political Science to study the issue and deliver a report. They did so and wrote the "Report on resolution of outstanding property claims between Cuba & the United States." More recently, on February 17, 2016, the Section on Taxation of the American Bar Association replied to a query by the Office of the Legal Adviser of the U.S. Department of State expressing its disagreement with the previous report.

Although one can't predict the atmosphere at the time of implementing this program, it is almost certain that the process of investment will be extended and confusion could develop from the discussion. This matter is of utmost importance because it is already happening. The sword of Damocles may end up in the wrong hands. Hopefully it will not be in the Halloween witch's.

---

[65] A list of claimants can be seen at https://www.justice.gov/sites/default/files/fcsc/docs/ccp-listofclaims.pdf.

An Appropriate Finale

Our last thought relates to the brief intervention of the leader maximum during the celebration of the 7th Congress of Cuba's Communist Party. Wearing his now perennial plaid shirt and sports top, he babbled a few sentences before going back to his autumnal existence. Although the system has yet to change, the era of his absolute power is over. He announced his upcoming 90th birthday and the likelihood of his near departure. After all, he is not immortal as we all suspected. He will leave behind a chaotic country, the product of his disastrous social and economic policies. The temptation is too strong: "*Adios, comandante*!"

LA INVERSIÓN EXTRANJERA EN CUBA SOCIALISTA:

GANANCIAS Y FUERZA LABORAL

José Alvarez, Ph.D.
Profesor Emérito, Universidad de la Florida

RESUMEN

Socialismo significa abolir la explotación del hombre por el hombre

Fidel Castro, discurso de Marzo 19, 1962

Este informe actualiza el titulado "La inversión extranjera en Cuba socialista: Ganancias reales inciertas para el capital extranjero y la continua explotación de la fuerza laboral". Fue preparado por José Álvarez por la Fundación para los Derechos Humanos en Cuba y publicado con toda intención el 1 de mayo de 2014. En el Día del Trabajo, los trabajadores de muchos países desfilan para exponer libremente sus demandas. No ha ocurrido en Cuba en los últimos 57 años.

En el primer párrafo de la versión anterior del presente informe se afirma que Cuba es un modelo de totalitarismo, opresión, discriminación y explotación. La explotación del trabajador se lleva a cabo con la complicidad de los capitalistas extranjeros que invierten en la Isla en busca de una ganancia rápida. A pesar de que la situación no ha cambiado, varios acontecimientos de los dos últimos años hacen necesario replantearse la cuestión. Ellos incluyen la renovación de relaciones diplomáticas con Estados Unidos que puede estar anunciando el fin del embargo económico a Cuba, además de la promulgación de varias leyes en Cuba y la celebración del 7° Congreso del Partido Comunista de Cuba. Algunos de estos sucesos tendrán un impacto en la inversión extranjera directa (IED) en Cuba.

La IED ha tenido una evolución tortuosa después de que Castro tomó el poder en 1959. Cuba realizaba la mayor parte de su comercio exterior con los países socialistas, y recibía grandes subvenciones de la Unión Soviética. No fue hasta 1982 que la legislación relativa a la inversión extranjera fue resucitada, pero fue engavetada hasta 1990, un año después de la caída del Muro de Berlín. El deseo de atraer capital extranjero -y lo poco que el Gobierno cubano está dispuesto a conceder por conseguirlo, se refleja en las numerosas leyes promulgadas desde ese momento hasta ahora.

El presente análisis adopta un enfoque holístico (integral) del proceso legislativo que ha tenido lugar en los últimos dos años. La razón es que inversión y mano de obra se entrelazan. Aunque la mayoría de los expertos alegan que el régimen cubano ha dado de nuevo "más de lo mismo", lo cierto es que ha habido algunas medidas tímidas aunque la explotación del trabajador continúa. Al comparar la antigua Ley número 77 de 1995, con el Decreto-Ley N° 313 de 2013 (ZEDM) y con la Ley N° 118 de 2014 que representa la última ley para la inversión extranjera, se pueden encontrar algunas diferencias menores en todas las áreas menos una: la explotación del trabajador.

Continúa el sistema de un solo empleador. Además de CUBALSE y ACOREC, hay disponibles otras 10 agencias de empleo para los inversores extranjeros en la Zona del Mariel. Su relación con el Estado sigue siendo la misma: toma de decisiones monopólica relativa a la contratación laboral, los salarios, la resolución de conflictos y otros asuntos.

Los inversores extranjeros se sienten atraídos a Cuba por una amplia oferta de mano de obra calificada y sumisa que se portará con toda tranquilidad y lo mejor que pueda con el fin de mantener sus puestos de trabajo. Por otra parte, existe un solo sindicato. Todos los trabajadores están agrupados en la Confederación de Trabajadores de Cuba (CTC), que funciona como parte integral del Gobierno y del Partido Comunista. Los que intentan o emprenden acciones encaminadas a establecer un sindicato independiente son objeto de enjuiciamiento y pueden terminar en la cárcel.

Otro mecanismo de control es el Código Penal, modificado en 2013 para adaptarlo a nuevas situaciones. La draconiana legislación incluye el permiso que otorga el artículo 87.1 para internar en pabellones psiquiátricos a aquellos que requieren dicho tratamiento. A muchos presos les aplicaron electroshocks como forma de tortura. El artículo 8.1 de la Ley de Procedimiento Penal autoriza a los Tribunales Municipales para determinar el grado de propensión a cometer un acto criminal de un ciudadano y actuar en consecuencia. Cuba es el único país del mundo que incluye dicho "delito" (la propensión a cometer un acto delictivo) en su Código Penal. La teoría de la desviación de Cesare Lombroso da pie a los Comités de Defensa de la Revolución (CDR) para enviar a cualquiera a la cárcel por ser "peligroso". Líderes laborales independientes y disidentes han sido enviados a la cárcel en virtud del artículo 8.1. A modo de ejemplo, William Reyes Mir, que pertenecía a un grupo no oficial en Banes, provincia de Holguín, fue detenido en septiembre de 2007 y condenado a dos años de trabajos forzados por "peligrosidad".

El nuevo Código Laboral también ayuda a domesticar la mano de obra para los inversores extranjeros. La nueva legislación mantiene la importancia del "expediente laboral" y no es extraño, porque esa carpeta contiene la información del trabajador desde el primer empleo hasta su jubilación. Se trata de un mecanismo de control de la mayor importancia para un régimen totalitario y una herramienta más para el inversor extranjero.

La legislación que prohíbe invertir a los cubanos residentes en la Isla ha suscitado protestas por su carácter discriminatorio. Uno de los que han protestado es Silvio Rodríguez, partidario inveterado del régimen. Su opción es el llamado "timbiriche" donde se vende algún tipo de alimento de origen dudoso, se arreglan las gomas ponchadas o se prestan servicios similares.

De todos los aspectos de las leyes y decretos principales, nuestro propósito es concentrarnos en estimar la magnitud de la explotación de los trabajadores nacionales por los inversores extranjeros bajo la dirección del Estado cubano. En primer lugar, todas las leyes y decretos-leyes especifican claramente que para los trabajadores cubanos y los extranjeros residentes permanentes en Cuba sólo hay un empleador; que las empresas extranjeras pagarán a la agencia estatal de empleo en moneda convertible, y esta pagará los trabajadores cubanos en moneda nacional. Si Karl Marx estuviera buscando el mejor ejemplo para ilustrar su teoría de la plusvalía, habría elegido la explotación de los trabajadores cubanos por el Estado socialista en complicidad con las empresas capitalistas extranjeras.

La trampa es doble. En primer lugar, el Estado permite la existencia de tres monedas diferentes con valores arbitrarios; y en segundo lugar, el Estado recauda con la moneda de mayor valor y paga al trabajador cubano con la moneda de menor valor. Por lo tanto, el trabajador es víctima de la broma (*trick*) y el Estado se queda con todas las golosinas (treat). Por ejemplo, con el tipo de cambio entre el peso cubano (CUP) / el peso convertible (CUC) / y el dólar de EE.UU. alrededor de 24CUP = 1CUC = US $1 por un CUC o dólar de salario devengado, el trabajador cubano recibe 1/25 o 4.16 % de la cantidad que la empresa extranjera pagó al Estado cubano por su salario. Así, el Estado cubano conserva (se apodera) del 95,84 % del salario. Esto se cumple para el sector exterior a excepción de la Zona de Desarrollo Especial del Mariel que recibe un tratamiento especial.

La legislación de la Zona Especial de Desarrollo del Mariel (ZEDM) contiene una tímida concesión. Aunque el mecanismo de la trampa sigue siendo el mismo, la asignación de dinero es ligeramente diferente. El Ministerio de Finanzas y Precios fijó la tasa de impuesto personal para los trabajadores de la ZEDM al 5 %. La ZEDM decidió que los trabajadores recibirían el 80 % del pago negociado entre el operador y la entidad cubana de contratación. El Ministerio de Trabajo y Seguridad Social establece el coeficiente para ajustar el salario de los trabajadores cubanos en "10“, lo que significa que la tasa de cambio entre el peso cubano (CUP) y el peso cubano convertible (CUC) para determinar la cantidad pagada a los trabajadores sería 10: 1.

Es obvio que toda la narración precedente abre la puerta a la falta de cumplimiento de los tratados internacionales por el gobierno de Cuba en complicidad de los inversores extranjeros. Estos incluyen, entre muchos otros, el Convenio sobre el trabajo forzoso de 1930, el Convenio sobre la abolición del trabajo forzado de 1957, el Convenio sobre la libre asociación y sindicación de 1948, el Convenio sobre la protección del salario de 1949, el Convenio sobre el derecho de sindicación y de negociación colectiva de 1949, el Convenio sobre la discriminación (en el empleo y la ocupación) de 1958, el Convenio sobre la política de empleo de 1964, y la Declaración Universal de Derechos Humanos, en especial su artículo 23.

Una pregunta queda sin respuesta: ¿Cómo se ha comportado en el pasado este sistema de inversiones y cuáles son las expectativas?

Es muy difícil llegar a una conclusión respecto de cuántas firmas y empresas ya están operando en Cuba. Además de la falta de detalles, hay contradicciones entre los informes de las organizaciones internacionales y de los economistas interesados.

La Conferencia de las Naciones Unidas sobre Comercio y Desarrollo (UNCTAD) estima una inversión extranjera acumulada de sólo US $ 215 millones para el período 1990-2009 (incluyendo $ 97 millones de 2007 a 2009). Las cifras reportadas por el Banco Mundial son casi idénticas: $ 210 millones para el período de 1994 a 2009 (y $ 85 millones en 2010). La Encuesta Coordinada de Inversión Directa del Fondo Monetario Internacional reporta $ 583 millones solo para España (finales de 2010). El Congreso Norteamericano sobre América Latina (NACLA) rebate estas cifras en un artículo escrito por Richard Feinberg, debido a que "chocan con la magnitud de las actividades de inversión extranjera que son fácilmente visibles en la Isla y que se registran en los informes anuales de las empresas internacionales que trabajan en Cuba". A continuación Feinberg se enfrasca en un ejercicio complejo con cifras proporcionadas por un consultor anónimo con acceso a los datos oficiales. Él reconoce que la falta de información tiene su origen en la "cultura del secretismo del gobierno cubano."

En cuanto a las oportunidades, estuvieron disponibles la última *Guía del Inversionista en Cuba* y la *Guía y Cartera de oportunidades para la inversión extranjera.* El Ministro de Comercio Exterior, Rodrigo Malmierca, anunció que Cuba estaba buscando $ 8.2 mil millones en inversión extranjera para 326 proyectos. Estas últimas cifras incluyen 80 proyectos más, pero un valor total de $ 500 millones menos que en 2014. Cuarenta de los 246 proyectos anunciados el año pasado se encuentran en "negociaciones avanzadas" y se han eliminado de la lista de este año.

Obviamente, incluso con la falta de datos fiables, Cuba no pudo alcanzar su meta de $ 8.2 millones el año pasado. ¿Qué hay de este año? El resultado predicho parece reducirse cuando se compara con otros países de la subregión del Caribe. En la edición más reciente del informe de la CEPAL se señala que después de caer a US $ 6.027 millones de dólares en 2014, la República Dominicana (DR) y Trinidad y Tobago (T & T) son los principales receptores en el Caribe, y absorben el 37% y el 23% de las entradas totales respectivamente. En el otro extremo, Cuba y Haití reciben sólo pequeñas cantidades de IED, a pesar de sus grandes poblaciones. Es interesante observar que la República Dominicana y Trinidad y Tobago recibieron el 60% de los US $ 6.027 millones de dólares, dejando US $ 2.41 mil millones para el resto de los países de la subregión del Caribe.

Los inversores extranjeros que buscan oportunidades en Cuba deben considerarlo muy en serio ya que el comportamiento pasado de Cuba parece indicar que invertir en Cuba no sólo podría resultar en un revés financiero grave para las empresas extranjeras, sino también podría terminar con una sentencia de cárcel para el empresario que se arriesga, como se muestra en el texto.

Con la posibilidad de invertir en Cuba después de que se levante el embargo, un tema olvidado se ha puesto de manifiesto una vez más. Su nombre es el "Programa de las reivindicaciones cubanas" y se refiere a las propiedades de ciudadanos estadounidenses expropiadas por el régimen de Castro en los primeros años de la revolución. Una lista actual contiene cerca de 7.000 reclamaciones. No mucho tiempo después de eso, el Servicio de Impuestos Internos autorizó a esas personas a utilizar lo que se llama "la pérdida en Cuba" y deducir una parte de su pérdida de sus impuestos federales. Las discusiones entre las agencias federales sobre cómo hacer frente a ese problema ya han comenzado. Cualquiera que sea la decisión que tome el Gobierno Federal, esta afectará a todas las partes interesadas, especialmente si una persona compró una propiedad que pertenece a uno de los demandantes.

Nuestro último pensamiento se refiere a la intervención breve de Fidel Castro durante la celebración del 7º Congreso del Partido Comunista de Cuba en abril de 2016. A pesar de que el sistema todavía está por cambiar, la era de su poder absoluto ha terminado. Anunció su próximo 90 cumpleaños y la probabilidad de su cercana partida. Dejará atrás un país sumido en el caos, producto de sus desastrosas políticas sociales y económicas. La tentación es demasiado fuerte: "¡Adiós, Comandante!"

Introducción

Socialismo significa abolir la explotación del hombre por el hombre

Fidel Castro, discurso de Marzo 19, 1962

Al igual que en la mayoría de los casos, Fidel Castro no estaba diciendo la verdad. El Estado socialista de Cuba es un ejemplo de libro de texto del totalitarismo, la opresión, la discriminación y la explotación. Como una paradoja irónica, el régimen cubano ejerce su poder absoluto sobre la clase obrera con la complicidad de los capitalistas extranjeros que invierten con el gobierno cubano en la Isla en busca de una ganancia rápida.

El primer párrafo de la versión original de este documento, fechado 1º de mayo de 2014, sigue siendo cierto hoy en día. Sin embargo, algunos acontecimientos que han tenido lugar durante los últimos dos años hacen que sea necesario reexaminar la cuestión con el fin de actualizarlo para la situación en Cuba. Algunos hechos incluyen:

- El 17 de diciembre de 2014, el presidente Obama y el presidente Castro anunciaron al mismo tiempo un nuevo rumbo en las relaciones entre Estados Unidos y Cuba. En los meses siguientes se llevaron a cabo varios cambios de política.
- El Secretario de Estado de EE.UU. eliminó a Cuba de la lista de países que patrocinan el terrorismo; delegaciones de ambos países llevaron a cabo una conferencia sobre cuestiones de derechos humanos; las dos embajadas se abrieron oficialmente; una comisión bilateral se estableció para hacer avanzar el proceso de normalización; se realizaron varias reuniones conjuntas para resolver problemas en diferentes áreas; y tuvo lugar el primer vuelo comercial para llevar la correspondencia a Cuba.
- El 29 de septiembre de 2015, se publicó en la *Gaceta Oficial de Cuba* No. 40 la Resolución 20/2015 del Ministerio de Trabajo y Seguridad Social, que contiene las normas que rigen la contratación de trabajadores nacionales por las empresas extranjeras que operan en Cuba.
- Los días 22 a 24 de marzo de 2016, el presidente Obama hizo una histórica visita a Cuba y pronunció un impresionante discurso que fue escuchado por el pueblo cubano.

- Los días 17 a 19 de abril de 2016, en Cuba se celebró el 7° Congreso del Partido Comunista. El canciller Bruno Rodríguez lanzó un ataque severo sobre la visita del Presidente Obama a la Isla, y la describió como un "ataque profundo a nuestras ideas, a nuestra historia, a nuestra cultura y a nuestros símbolos". Contrariamente a lo esperado de que se instalaría un liderazgo más joven, el presidente Raúl Castro y los otros miembros de la "histórica" vieja guardia permanecieron en el poder.

Directa o indirectamente, estos acontecimientos podrían repercutir en el futuro desarrollo de las inversiones extranjeras con el gobierno cubano en la Isla. De especial importancia es el potencial levantamiento completo del embargo económico de EE.UU. contra Cuba, que ampliaría las oportunidades de inversión con el Estado cubano y contribuiría a las arcas del gobierno cubano sin ningún beneficio directo para el pueblo cubano.

El objetivo de esta actualización es investigar lo que ha sucedido en el ámbito de la inversión extranjera desde nuestro informe publicado el 1 de mayo de 2014 y también examinar algunas consideraciones sobre la posible repercusión de las relaciones económicas con Estados Unidos sobre el tipo y cantidad de inversiones de Estados Unidos en la Isla.

Evolución de la ley cubana para la inversión extranjera

Las presiones ejercidas contra los empresarios extranjeros que desean invertir en Cuba son terribles, son increíbles... son muy fuertes, porque quieren descarrilar a toda costa el esfuerzo económico del país, como parte de su plan integral para destruir la Revolución.

Fidel Castro, discurso de Agosto 5, 1994

Después de que Fidel Castro tomó el poder en 1959, la inversión extranjera llegó a ser prácticamente inexistente en Cuba. A los ojos del régimen cubano esta no era necesaria ya que Cuba contaba con abundantes recursos heredados de los regímenes anteriores antes de convertirse en miembro especial del Consejo de Ayuda Mutua Económica (CAME) a partir de 1972 hasta su disolución en 1991.

Sin embargo, con el Decreto-Ley Nº 50 de 15 de febrero de 1982, se resucitó la inversión extranjera mediante la regulación de las asociaciones económicas entre el gobierno cubano y las empresas extranjeras. Debido a algunos problemas inherentes a la desconfianza, la primera asociación no se materializó hasta 1990, un año después de la caída del muro de Berlín. El impacto de la desaparición de sus principales socios comerciales resultó desastroso para la economía cubana.

El deseo de atraer capital extranjero se refleja en la nueva Constitución de 1992, en cuyo artículo 23 se reconoce la propiedad de las empresas mixtas y las asociaciones económicas. El 21 de abril de 1994, fue establecido el Ministerio para la Inversión Extranjera y la Colaboración Económica (MINVEC) para promover y regular dichas actividades.

El 5 de septiembre de 1995, la Asamblea Nacional de Cuba promulgó una nueva Ley de Inversión Extranjera N ° 77 que otorga mayor seguridad a los extranjeros que deseen invertir en la Isla. Después de un flujo de capital inicial, los siguientes veinte años fueron testigos de una dramática disminución neta del número de empresas establecidas. Se hizo evidente que la legislación de 1995 hacía poco para ayudar a aliviar la deprimente situación económica del país.

Bajo el presidente Raúl Castro, la Asamblea Nacional de Cuba promulgó la Ley N ° 118 de 16 de abril de 2014 destinada a corregir la falta de incentivos presentes en legislaciones anteriores. Nuestro trabajo original investigaba el grado en que la Ley Nº 118 podría cumplir con su objetivo de atraer un flujo de capital extranjero necesario para la Isla. También se refería al método de contratación de los empleados nacionales, que sufren una brutal explotación. Esa característica todavía es válida hoy en día.

Dicho aspecto de la legislación sobre inversiones extranjeras se reiteró con la publicación en la Gaceta Oficial de Cuba No. 40 de 29 de septiembre de 2015, de la Resolución N ° 20/2015 del Ministerio de Trabajo y Seguridad Social, que contiene las regulaciones relacionadas con los cubanos que solicitan trabajo en ciertos tipos de empresas extranjeras.

Un enfoque integrado

El gobierno cubano debe revisar sus leyes de inversión extranjera para eliminar la dependencia a las agencias de empleo controladas por el Estado y otros impedimentos para el activismo laboral... Los inversores extranjeros en Cuba deben utilizar su influencia con el gobierno cubano para presionar para que Cuba cumpla los tratados internacionales en materia de derechos humanos y derechos laborales que se ha comprometido a respetar.

Human Rights Watch, *La maquinaria represiva de Cuba*[66]

Las medidas económicas relativas a la inversión extranjera aprobadas por el régimen de Raúl Castro no deben considerarse de forma aislada.

Este análisis adopta un enfoque holístico (integrado) del proceso legislativo que ha tenido lugar entre 2013 y 2015, destinado a contribuir al esfuerzo para sacar al país de la situación económica peor de los 57 años en que el liderazgo cubano ha gobernado el país. Uno tiene que comprender tanto la legislación sobre inversiones como la relacionada con la fuerza de trabajo, ya que están entrelazadas.

En la Tabla 1 se enumeran las medidas dirigidas a atraer inversiones extranjeras directas y a proporcionarles una fuerza de trabajo complaciente.

---

[66] https://www.hrw.org/reports/1999/cuba/index.htm#TopOfPage

Tabla 1. Enfoque integrado del proceso legislativo concerniente a inversiones extranjeras y el tema de la explotación de la fuerza de trabajo cubana por los inversores extranjeros, selección de medidas 2013-2015.

Fecha	Organo legislativo	Medida legislativa	Objetivo de la legislación
Legislación relativa a inversiones extranjeras			
Septiembre 23, 2013	Consejo de Estado	Decreto Ley No. 313	Crea la Zona especial de desarrollo de Mariel (ZEDM)
Septiembre 23, 2013	Consejo de Ministros	Decreto No. 316	Definiciones y regulaciones relativas a la ZEDM
Abril 16, 2014	Asamblea Nacional del Poder Popular	Ley No. 118	Nueva Ley de inversiones extranjeras
Legislación destinada a suministrar una fuerza laboral disciplinada			
Junio 25, 2013	Consejo de Estado	Decreto-Ley No. 310	Cambia partes del código penal y de la ley de procedimiento penal
Junio 17, 2014	Asamblea Nacional del Poder Popular	Ley No. 116	Nuevo Código Laboral
Junio 17, 2014	Ministerio de trabajo y seguridad social	Resolución No. 29	Aprueba los informes, modelos y registros que deben llevar las empresas según el Código Laboral
Septiembre 29, 2015	Ministerio de Trabajo y Seguridad Social	Resolución No. 20	Normas y procedimientos para el pago a trabajadores nacionales en empresas extranjeras.

[a] Fecha de publicación en la *Gaceta Oficial de Cuba.*

Actual legislación cubana para la inversión extranjera

Nuestro Movimiento 26 de Julio nunca ha pedido la nacionalización de las inversiones extranjeras... Nacionalizar nunca puede ser tan gratificante como el tipo correcto de inversión privada, nacional y extranjera, dirigida a diversificar nuestra economía... Nuestra revolución es tanto moral como política.

Fidel Castro, Look, Febrero 4, 1958

Las cuatro leyes más importantes en materia de inversión extranjera incluyen: el Decreto-Ley No. 313 de 23 de septiembre de 2013 que creó la Zona Especial de Desarrollo del Mariel (ZDEM) y su decreto complementario No. 316 de la misma fecha que contiene las definiciones y regulaciones relacionadas con la ZEDM, la Ley para la inversión extranjera No. 118 de 16 de abril de 2014, y la Resolución Nº 20 del Ministerio de Trabajo y Seguridad Social, promulgada el 29 de septiembre de 2015. Las cuatro se apoyan en cambios realizados en el Código Penal en 2013, y un nuevo y muy esperado Código Laboral de 2014, lo que ayuda a cumplir el objetivo de proporcionar una fuerza de trabajo complaciente a los inversores extranjeros.

A pesar de que en la nueva legislación se contempla un modesto aumento en la flexibilidad, la lista de la Tabla 2 sigue otorgando las concesiones anteriores relativas al capital y un ligero cambio para algunos trabajadores, aunque el Estado muestra un total desprecio por las necesidades de los trabajadores nacionales. En lenguaje llano, el régimen cubano ha dado de nuevo "más de lo mismo".

Tabla 2. Comparación de características de la Ley No. 77 de 1995, el Decreto-Ley No. 313 de 2013 y la Ley No. 118 de 2014.

Legislación		
Ley No. 77 de 5/9/1995 (Anterior Ley de inversiones extranjeras)	Decreto-Ley No. 313 de 23/9/2013 (Zona especial de desarrollo – Mariel)	Ley No. 118 de 16/4/2014 (Nueva Ley de inversiones extranjeras)
Lugar de inicio del proceso		
Ministerio para la inversión extranjera y la colaboración económica (MINVEC) (Art. 23.1)	Oficina de la Zona especial de desarrollo de Mariel (Art. 6, Art. 9)	Consejo de Ministros, tras consulta con el Ministerio de Comercio Exterior e inversiones extranjeras (Art. 11)
Aprobación final		
Consejo Ejecutivo del Consejo de Ministros (Art. 23.5)	Consejo de Ministros (Art. 11)	En dependencia de la inversión: - Consejo de Estado - Consejo de Ministros - Unidad central autorizada (Art. 21.1-4)
Tipos de inversiones		
- Empresas mixtas - Firmas solo con capital extranjero - Contrato de asociación económica internacional (Art. 12)	Por inversores nacionales o extranjeros como usuarios o titulares de licencia (Art. 17, 23)	Sin cambios (Art. 13.1)
Áreas abiertas		
Todas excepto salud, educación y fuerzas armadas (Art. 10)	Las relativas al desarrollo de la zona (Art. 5)	Sin cambios desde la Ley No. 77 (Art. 11.1)
Inversores extranjeros		
Sí, en todas las formas	Sin cambios	Sin cambios
Cubanos residentes en el extranjero		
No se menciona	Sí, como extranjeros, pero no se menciona explícitamente (Art. 23)	Sí, como extranjeros, pero no se menciona explícitamente (Art. 2.l)

Cubanos residentes en la isla		
No se menciona	Como supra (Art. 23)	Solo en empresas mixtas o asociaciones económicas internacionales (Art. 2.m)
Repatriación de ganancias		
Sí, sin restricciones ni pago, pero solo extranjeros (Art. 8)	No se menciona pero se asume igual que arriba	Sin cambios (Art. 9.1)
Obligaciones fiscales		
- 30% de retorno neto (Art. 39.a) - 50% en caso de explotación de recurso natural (Art. 39.b)	-Exento en varios casos (Art. 57) -12% impuesto sobre ganancia de capital -1% pago de impuesto sobre ventas y servicios -14% de salarios como aporte a seguridad social (Art. 58) (Decreto No. 316 del Consejo de Ministros)	- 15% del retorno neto (Art. 36.1) -50% en caso de explotación de recurso natural (Art. 36.4) - Nuevas exenciones (Art. 36.2, 36.3, 36.4, 37.2, 38.2. 39) -Se añaden bonificaciones en casos específicos (Art. 37.1, 38.1)
Adquisición del estatuto legal		
Tras registro en la Cámara de Comercio de Cuba (Art. 13.7)	Tras autorización por el Consejo de Ministros o el Director General de la Zona (Art. 24)	Tras inscripción en el Registro Comercial (Art. 14.6, 15.5, 16.2)
Protección contra la expropiación		
Salvo por bien público o interés social (Art. 3)	No se menciona explícitamente	Según la Constitución, la legislación vigente, acuerdos internacionales y debida compensación de mutuo acuerdo (Art. 4.1)

Explotación de la fuerza de trabajo

En un sistema socialista no existe la explotación del hombre por el hombre

Fidel Castro, discurso de Marzo 19, 1962

En una legislación tras otra, la mayoría de los asuntos relacionados con la contratación, el despido y la compensación de la fuerza de trabajo se ha mantenido sin cambios. Crear esta dependencia económica de los ciudadanos al estado es un pilar fundamental del totalitarismo. Admitir colaborar con esa premisa comunista muestra que las intenciones tras una apertura económica de Cuba bajo las circunstancias actuales distan mucho de la retórica de que el capitalismo traería la democracia y los derechos humanos. En esta sección se muestra el grado en que los trabajadores domésticos son explotados por el Estado cubano con la complicidad de los inversores extranjeros

Un sistema de un solo empleador

El gobierno de Cuba es el único proveedor de trabajadores y es el que toma las decisiones sobre contratación, sueldos y salarios, disciplina, despidos, vacaciones, seguridad social y muchos otros. Con el cierre de la empresa estatal CUBALSE (Cuba al Servicio del Extranjero) en mayo de 2009, parece que las únicas agencias estatales de empleo disponibles para los inversores extranjeros son ACOREC (*Agencia de Contratación a Representaciones Comerciales*), y AUSA (*Almacenes Universales, S.A.*).

En el caso de la Zona Especial de Desarrollo - Mariel (ZEDM), hay 12 agencias de empleo; a saber: Agencia Almacenes Universales SA, Grupo BioCubaFarma, Empresa Empleadora de la Construcción, Tecnosime, Empresa de Servicios de Ingeniería Eléctrica Cubana SA (Siecsa), Petroempleo, CUBATABACO, Empresa de Servicios Especializados de las Comunicaciones (Delta), Turempleo, Empresa Empleadora del Transporte (Agemport), Corporación Cubaron S.A., e Inversiones Gamma S.A.

Monopolio en la toma de decisiones

El Estado cubano dicta las calificaciones que un trabajador nacional debe tener, y los pasos que debe seguir, con el fin de solicitar un empleo en una empresa extranjera. La Tabla 3 muestra algunas generalidades al respecto.

Tabla 3. Selección de criterios relativos a la contratación de trabajadores nacionales por firmas extranjeras según Ley No. 77 de 2005, Decreto-Ley No. 313 de 2013, Ley No. 118 de 2014, Decreto No. 316 de 2013 y Resolución No. 20 de 2015.

Características de la legislación				
Ley No. 77 de 5/9/1995 (Antigua Ley de inversiones extranjeras)	Decreto-Ley No. 313 de 23/9/2013 (Zona especial de desarrollo de Mariel)	Ley No. 118 de 16/4/2014 (Nueva Ley de inversiones extranjeras)	Decreto No. 316 de 23/9/2013 (Regulaciones para la ZEDM)	Resolución No. 20 de 29/9/2015 (Regulaciones del Ministerio de Trabajo y Seguridad Social)
Contratación de mano de obra				
Una agencia empleadora estatal con muchas facultades (Art. 33, 34)	Sin cambios (Art. 31, 32)	Sin cambios (Art. 30.1- 30.4)	Sin cambios (Art. 36)	Sin cambios (Art. 2b)
Salarios de la mano de obra				
Pagado en pesos cubanos; menos del 2.5% de lo que la firma extranjera paga por ellos a la agencia empleadora estatal	-El Ministerio de Finanzas y Precios fija la tasa de impuesto personal para trabajadores de la ZEDM al 5%[67] -Los trabajadores reciben el 80% del pago[68].	Sin cambios	Véase Columna 2	Pagado en pesos cubanos (Art. 22) Las mismas regulaciones (Art. 8)

[67] Ministry of Finance and Prices, Resolution No. 139/2014, Official Gazette, May 7, 2014.

[68] "Régimen de contratación en zona especial de Mariel beneficiará a trabajadores." *Cuba Debate*, April 14, 2014.

	-El coeficiente por ajuste salarial es 10:1.[69]			
Creación de un fondo de incentivos para los trabajadores				
Sí (Art. 32)	Contribuciones destinadas al mantenimiento de la zona (Art. 44)	Sí (Art. 29.1)	Aparentemente no están presentes.	Aparentemente no están presentes.
Resolución de conflictos				
En tribunales populares designados por el Consejo de Gobierno del Tribunal Supremo (Art. 57, 58)	-Corte cubana de arbitraje del comercio internacional (Art. 45) - Director General de la oficina (Art. 46)	En dependencia del caso: -Sala de lo económico del Tribunal Provincial Popular (Art. 60.3, 60.4, 61)	El Director General de la Oficina y la Agencia de la Administración Central o la entidad competente (Art. 51)	El jefe de la Agencia empleadora estatal (Art. 16).

Como se muestra en la Tabla 3, la nueva ley de inversión extranjera mantiene el monopolio del Estado cubano en la toma de decisiones presente en legislaciones anteriores.

El Decreto Ley No. 313 establece que los trabajadores cubanos o extranjeros de la Zona de Mariel deben ser residentes permanentes cubanos y deben ser contratados por una entidad empleadora diseñada a tal efecto por el Estado cubano (artículo 31).

El artículo 32 especifica que las excepciones a la situación de residencia y contratación son el personal técnico y administrativo con la autorización previa de las correspondientes autoridades cubanas.

El Decreto N ° 316 del Consejo de Ministros que complementa dicha ley regula todos los aspectos de la relación entre la entidad extranjera y la mano de obra cubana.

El artículo 35 especifica que los residentes permanentes cubanos o extranjeros deben establecer una relación con la agencia empleadora del Estado antes de ser elegibles para el trabajo.

69 "Régimen de contratación en Zona Especial de Mariel", "Cuba anuncia reglas salariales para empleados de la Zona Franca del Mariel" (*El Nuevo Herald*, May 10, 2014; and Ministry of Labor and Social Security's Resolución No. 14/2014, Oficial Gafete, May 7, 2014.

Suministrar una fuerza laboral sumisa

Es vergonzoso que muchos inversores extranjeros se sientan atraídos por la mano de obra cubana que tendrán a su disposición. Es un grupo pacífico, disciplinado, "domesticado" y educado de trabajadores donde las huelgas son desconocidas y que trabajará de la mejor manera posible para mantener sus puestos. Un lugar de trabajo libre de problemas es sin duda un importante incentivo para invertir en Cuba Socialista.

Un solo sindicato (controlado por el Estado)

Los trabajadores cubanos no tienen el apoyo de su presunta representante sindical porque es parte del Estado. La Central de Trabajadores de Cuba (CTC), el único sindicato reconocido, no es una organización legítima de los trabajadores; es un apéndice del gobierno y del Partido Comunista. Se invita al lector a buscar un caso que muestre a la CTC en pie contra el régimen cubano para defender a un solo trabajador. Por otra parte, desde que la revolución tomó el poder en 1959, los desfiles del Primero de Mayo son manifestaciones de presunto apoyo unánime de los trabajadores al régimen en lugar de una oportunidad de presentar sus demandas. ¡Ni una sola en más de 57 años!

Irónicamente, el artículo 54 de la Constitución de 1976 (modificada en 1992) garantiza a los trabajadores los derechos de reunión, manifestación y asociación. Las organizaciones de masas y sociales disponen de todas las facilidades para el desenvolvimiento de dichas actividades en las que los miembros tienen amplia libertad de palabra y opinión, basadas en el derecho irrestricto a la iniciativa y a la crítica. Obviamente, como en muchos otros casos, el régimen cubano está violando su propia ley.

El 21 de octubre de 2013, el régimen cubano estaba buscando largas penas de prisión contra los líderes laborales independientes Vladimir Morera y Jorge Ramírez Calderón, de la "Federación Cubana de Trabajadores Independientes", una entidad no estatal no reconocida por el gobierno. Aunque encarcelados desde septiembre de 2012, el régimen estaba pidiendo ocho y cinco años más, respectivamente. Los cargos incluían desobediencia, desorden público y desacato. Ambos fueron puestos en libertad por la mediación de la Iglesia Católica y partieron hacia Estados Unidos en marzo de 2016.

Modificación del Código Penal

El 29 de mayo de 2013, del Consejo de Estado de Cuba promulgó el Decreto - Ley No. 310 que cambia partes del Código Penal y de la Ley de Procedimiento Penal, publicado en la *Gaceta Oficial de la República de Cuba* el 25 de junio de 2013. Su principal objetivo es adaptar el

Código a las condiciones cambiantes debido a las reformas económicas que exigen un mayor énfasis en la prevención y el castigo de la actividad criminal.

El artículo 87.1 permite el uso de la reclusión psiquiátrica para aquellos que requieren dicho tratamiento. El artículo 8.1 de la Ley de Procedimiento Penal mantiene que a los tribunales populares municipales se les permite determinar el grado de propensión de un ciudadano a cometer un acto criminal y actuar en consecuencia. Cuba es el único país del mundo que incluye dichos delitos en su Código Penal. Cuba es también un país que utiliza medios psiquiátricos para interrogar y torturar a los presos políticos, según lo documentado por Brown y Lago.

Es muy interesante que el artículo 8.1 extienda a la actividad política la vieja teoría de la desviación propuesta por el italiano Cesare Lombroso. De acuerdo con su teoría de la antropología criminal, la criminalidad se hereda y los "criminales natos" podrían ser identificados por defectos físicos, que confirman a un delincuente como salvaje o atávico. En el caso de Cuba, esos "criminales natos" son identificados por los Comités de Defensa de la Revolución o las fuerzas represivas, que no necesitan dar más detalles sobre teorías antropológicas complejas. No hace falta añadir que líderes de sindicatos independientes y disidentes han sido enviados a la cárcel en virtud del artículo 8.1. Uno de ellos fue William Reyes Mir, que pertenecía a un grupo político no oficial en Banes, provincia de Holguín. Reyes fue detenido en septiembre de 2007 y condenado a dos años de trabajos forzados por "peligrosidad".

Un nuevo Código Laboral

La Asamblea Nacional aprobó una nueva Ley del Código Laboral el 20 de diciembre de 2013 para sustituir a la promulgada en 1984. Sin embargo, no fue publicada en la Gaceta Oficial hasta el 17 de junio de 2014. En general, el nuevo Código es muy similar al viejo. Comparten la mayor parte de las restricciones. Al igual que su antecesor, su principal objetivo es mantener a los trabajadores a raya. Las medidas restrictivas y represivas contra los trabajadores mencionadas en otras partes de este documento constituyen pruebas fehacientes de violaciones del régimen de su propio Código Laboral.

La nueva legislación mantiene la importancia del "expediente laboral" y no es extraño, porque esa carpeta contiene la información relacionada con el trabajador desde su primer empleo hasta la jubilación. Se trata de un mecanismo de control de la mayor importancia para un régimen totalitario.

La pertinencia de un enfoque integrado es apoyada de nuevo por la Resolución N ° 29 del Ministerio de Trabajo y Seguridad Social (MTSS), publicada en la *Gaceta Oficial* el 17 de junio de 2014. Esta Resolución invoca el Código Laboral como la legislación que rige al MTSS a cumplir los registros, formularios y otra información que deben mantener las empresas. El excesivo número de documentos tiene el objetivo principal de tener a mano toda la información (tanto para el trabajo como para la política) de cada trabajador del país.

Una discriminación flagrante

A la mayor parte de los cubanos en la Isla les molesta la repetición de la escena que tuvo lugar en 1977 y en años posteriores, cuando el régimen cubano, por falta de dinero en efectivo, desplegó la alfombra roja para que los exiliados cubanos llevaran a Cuba presentes y dinero en efectivo para sus familias y amigos. La nueva ley de inversión extranjera, así como la creación de la zona de desarrollo especial del Mariel, no sólo explotan a los trabajadores cubanos con la complicidad de las empresas extranjeras, sino que los discriminan al no permitirles el mismo privilegio concedido a sus compatriotas que viven en el extranjero.

Las quejas han surgido desde el principio. La estrella de la Nueva Trova, Silvio Rodríguez, un inveterado partidario del régimen, expresó su frustración en su blog acerca de la exclusión de los residentes cubanos de los grandes negocios. Y se hace la pregunta embarazosa: "¿Cuándo vamos, los que nos quedamos en Cuba para defender la Revolución, a disfrutar de los mismos derechos?" Creo que el señor Rodríguez merece una respuesta: "Nunca, a menos que se trate de invertir en los llamados 'timbiriches' que venden alimentos de origen dudoso, cogen ponches a los neumáticos o prestan un servicio similar". Huelga decir, que él no tiene necesidad de que le envíen dinero los familiares en el extranjero. La razón es simple: el régimen al que ha apoyado durante tantos años no permite cubanos ricos. Eso es algo reservado sólo para los extranjeros, funcionarios públicos seleccionados y sus familiares y, por supuesto, los nacionales cubanos que viven en libertad en tierras extranjeras.

Cálculo de la magnitud de la explotación

Se puede decir que Cuba ya no es una República, sino una monarquía hereditaria y que Batista puede nombrarse a sí mismo rey. Él puede desmembrar el territorio nacional y vender una provincia a un país extranjero como hizo Napoleón con Luisiana. . . Todas estas medidas serían legales y habría que encarcelar a todos aquellos que se opongan a ellas, del mismo modo que ahora tratan de hacer conmigo. He puesto ejemplos extremos para mostrar cuán triste y humillante es nuestra situación actual. ¡Y pensar que todos estos poderes absolutos están en las manos de hombres verdaderamente capaces de vender nuestro país, junto con todos sus ciudadanos!

Fidel Castro, *La historia me absolverá* (1953)[70]

Todas las leyes y decretos- leyes especifican claramente que para los trabajadores cubanos y los extranjeros residentes permanentes en Cuba sólo hay un empleador; que las empresas extranjeras pagarán a la agencia estatal empleadora en moneda convertible, y esta pagará a los trabajadores cubanos en moneda nacional a un tipo de cambio fijado arbitrariamente, de 25 CUP = 1 CUC = US $ 1.

Según la Ley de inversiones extranjeras

Si Karl Marx estuviera buscando el ejemplo más ilustrativo para su teoría de la plusvalía, habría elegido la explotación de los trabajadores cubanos por el Estado socialista en complicidad con las empresas capitalistas extranjeras.

La trampa es doble. En primer lugar, el Gobierno permite la existencia de tres monedas diferentes con valores arbitrarios; y en segundo lugar, el Gobierno cobra con la moneda de mayor valor y paga al trabajador con la moneda de menor valor. Por lo tanto, el trabajador sufre el truco (trick) y el Estado se queda con todas las golosinas (treat). Por ejemplo, con el tipo de cambio entre el peso cubano (CUP) / el peso convertible (CUC) / y el dólar de EE.UU. alrededor

[70] Castro's alleged self-defense during the trail for the attack on the Moncada barracks appears in numerous publications. The one selected can be found in https://www.marxists.org/history/cuba/archive/castro/1953/10/16.htm.

de 25 CUP = 1 CUC = US $ 1, para cualquier CUC o dólar de salario dado, el trabajador cubano recibe 1/25 o 4 % de la cantidad que la empresa extranjera pagó al Estado cubano por su salario. Así, el Estado cubano conserva (se apodera de) el 96 % del sueldo. Este método de pago se sigue aplicando en el país, pero se creó uno diferente para la Zona Especial de Desarrollo del Mariel.

A partir de numerosos testimonios, he seleccionado uno que no deja dudas sobre la veracidad de lo anterior: el Gobierno de España, uno de los principales participantes. Patrocinado por la Oficina Económica y Comercial de la Embajada de España en Cuba, Gregorio Dávila Díaz escribió un artículo titulado "Mercado de Trabajo de Cuba para las empresas extranjeras". El autor explica que el salario se compone de tres partes: el salario mínimo aprobado por el Ministerio de Trabajo y Seguridad Social; un incremento que refleja el estatus profesional (calificación y experiencia); y un coeficiente de desconocida metodología que se aplica en función de la categoría (Tabla 4).

Tabla 4. Metodología y procedimientos ad hoc para calcular salarios mensuales para trabajadores nacionales en firmas extranjeras en Cuba, 2014

Categoría del empleado	Salario mínimo mensual por trabajador		Coeficiente[c]	US$ de salario mensual que se apropia el Estado	
	Peso Cubano (CUP)[a]	(Equivalencia en US$)[b]		Total recibido por la agencia estatal (US$)[d]	Parte para la empresa empleadora estatal (US$)[e]
No calificado	150	5.66	1,7797	266.96	261.30
Baja calif.	205	7.74	1,6755	343.48	335.74
Mediana calif.	260	9.81	1,6157	420.08	410.27
Alta calif.	335	12.64	1,5658	524.54	511.90
Ejecutivos	410	15.47	1,5342	629.02	613.55
Directores	435	16.42	1,5261	663.85	647.44

[a] Suma pagada en pesos cubanos por la Agencia empleadora estatal al trabajador.

[b] A una tasa de 26.5 pesos cubanos por 1 US dólar. Por ejemplo: 150/26.5 = US$ 5.66. (http:www.xe.com/currencyconverter/convert/?From=USD&To=CUP), última visita mayo 16, 2016.

[c] Coeficiente de metodología desconocida dirigido a llenar los huecos por niveles de grados y experiencia.

[d] Suma pagada en dólares de EE.UU por la firma extranjera a la Agencia empleadora estatal. Por ejemplo: 150 x 1.7797 = US$ 266.96.

[e] Diferencia en dólares de EE.UU. entre lo que recibe la Agencia empleadora estatal de la firma extranjera y lo que paga al trabajador. Por ejemplo: US$ 266.96 – 5.66 = US$ 261.30.

Al tipo de cambio vigente en el momento en que se publicó la versión original de este documento, de 26,5 pesos cubanos por 1 dólar, un empleado no calificado recibiría US $ 5.66 al mes (150 / 26,5), que es de 2.12 % (5.66 / 267) de lo que la empresa paga por él / ella en los salarios de la época. El porcentaje recibido por los trabajadores aumenta ligeramente hasta un máximo de 2,47 % (16,42 / 663,85) para la Administración.

Aunque es imposible predecir cuántos trabajadores serán contratados bajo las dos nuevas iniciativas, el estudio de Dávila Díaz mencionado anteriormente utiliza 24.190 trabajadores empleados por empresas extranjeras en el momento de su estudio. Aunque la agencia estatal recibe otros ingresos de cargos adicionales, la Tabla 5 cuantifica la explotación de los trabajadores en diferentes niveles de empleo.

Tabla 5. Explotación de los trabajadores a distintos niveles de empleo, 2014

Nivel de empleo[a]	Salarios mensuales por unidad[b] (US$)	Ingreso/año (US$)
1	398	4,777
25,000	9,952,525	119,430,300
30,000	11,913,030	143,316,360
35,000	13,933,535	167,202,420
40,000	15,924,040	191,088,480
45,000	17,914,545	217,974,540
50,000	19,905,050	238,860,600

[a] Número de trabajadores nacionales empleados en determinado momento.

[b] La unidad se define por las seis categorías de empleo. En aras de simplificar, se asume la siguiente distribución: No calificados: 30%; Baja calificación: 20%; Mediana calificación: 20%; Alta calificación: 15%; Ejecutivos: 10%; y Directores: 5%. Por ejemplo, en el primer caso, por 33 obreros no calificados el gobierno recibe US$261.29, pero se asume que solo el 30% están en esa categoría (0.30 x 261.29 = 78.39), y así sucesivamente.

Los cálculos revelan un resultado sorprendente. La agencia estatal de empleo, al manejar de entre 25.000 y 50.000 trabajadores con la distribución de las calificaciones asumidas, puede obtener un beneficio neto de entre US $ 119 y US $ 239 millones por año. La cifra es más bien conservadora. Al suponer que el salario medio de un asistente de ventas fue CP 382,01 mensuales (identificado en una tabla salarial), dos investigadores llegaron a la conclusión de que la agencia empleadora estatal estaba recibiendo alrededor de US $ 256 millones por año cuando se consideraron todos los empleados. Esa cifra es superior a los flujos anuales de nuevas inversiones extranjeras en Cuba durante el período 1993-1998 (aproximadamente US $ 225 millones).

Obviamente, al menos en ese momento, el régimen cubano cosechaba más beneficios de la explotación de los trabajadores que a partir del valor de las nuevas inversiones extranjeras que llegan a la isla. No hay razones para creer que la situación va a cambiar en la nueva Ley. Y no lo hizo, como se explica a continuación.

Para la Zona Especial de Desarrollo del Mariel

Aunque todavía no han podido conservar su plusvalía, los trabajadores de la Zona Especial de Desarrollo del Mariel (ZEDM) funcionan bajo un régimen ligeramente diferente. Los artículos 31, 32 y 33 de la Sección Tercera del Decreto -Ley No. 313 que creó la ZEDM explican el "Régimen Especial del Trabajo " en ese lugar. En ellos se repite que todos los trabajadores deben ser residentes permanentes de Cuba, y que son contratados a través de la agencia estatal de empleo. La Resolución N ° 20/2015 cubre el tema de los trabajadores.

En la primera quincena de mayo de 2014, el gobierno cubano anunció la definición de los parámetros que sólo se aplicarían a la ZEDM. Aunque el mecanismo de la trampa sigue siendo el mismo, la asignación de dinero es ligeramente diferente:

- El Ministerio de Finanzas y Precios fijó la tasa de impuesto personal para los trabajadores en la ZEDM al 5 %.
- El ZEDM decidió que los trabajadores recibirían el 80 % del pago negociado entre el operador y la entidad empleadora cubana.
- El Ministerio de Trabajo y Seguridad Social establece el coeficiente para ajustar el salario de los trabajadores cubanos de "10", lo que significa que la tasa de cambio entre el peso cubano (CUP) y el peso convertible cubano (CUC) para determinar la cantidad pagada a trabajadores sería de 10: 1, en lugar de 24: 1 aplicado en el resto del país.

Una trifecta de explotación

Trifecta se define como " una apuesta en la que el jugador pronostica los tres primeros lugares en una carrera en el orden correcto". En este caso, el orden "correcto" en el orden cronológico y, tal vez, en el grado de explotación, de más a menos, sería la siguiente: un obrero del sector estatal normal, una empresa en el sector de la inversión extranjera, y la Zona Especial de Desarrollo del Mariel (ZEDM).

Un ejemplo hipotético muestra cómo se calculan los pagos para el personal cubano que trabaja en la ZEDM. El acuerdo entre la agencia estatal de empleo y la empresa extranjera establece este salario a 1.000 CUP por mes. En el cálculo de la división 80-20 entre el trabajador y la agencia estatal de empleo, el trabajador recibiría 800 CUP (1000 x 0,8) y la agencia estatal de empleo CUP 200 (1000 x 0,2). El coeficiente de 10 aumentaría su salario a 8.000 CUP por mes (800 x 10). El impuesto personal (5 %) sobre una renta de 8.000 CUP sería 400 CUP, dejando un sueldo neto de 7.600 CUP. El trabajador necesita convertir los pesos a CUC (24 CUP: 1CUC, que es la tasa de cambio actual). Por lo tanto, recibe 317 CUC (7600 / 24) de la cantidad pagada por el inversor extranjero. Los restantes 683 CUC van a la Agencia Empleadora Estatal. En por ciento, el trabajador recibe el 31,7 % (317/1000) y el Estado se queda con el 68,3 % restante. (Tabla 6).

Tabla 6. Comparación de salario mensual entre dos clases distintas de trabajadores cubanos en empresa mixta y en la ZEDM.

Empresa mixta		ZEDM	
Parte para el trabajador	Parte para la Agencia emp. estatal	Parte para el trabajador	Parte para la Agencia emp. estatal
2.47%	97.53%	31.7%	68.3%

La mayoría de la gente está familiarizada con el libro de George Orwell *Rebelión en la granja*. Los cerdos que controlan el gobierno en la novela emitieron una proclama: "Todos los animales son iguales, pero algunos animales son más iguales que otros". A pesar de que el precepto está concebido para la clase gobernante, puede utilizarse para nuestro ejemplo de la explotación de la clase obrera por el Estado cubano: "Todos los empleados son explotados, pero algunos empleados son más explotados que los demás".

La Tabla 7 revela que dicha declaración es correcta y en contradicción con su Constitución, cuyo artículo 9 declara: "a) el Estado cumple la voluntad del pueblo trabajador y sostiene la ideología y las normas de convivencia y de conducta típicas de la sociedad libre de explotación del hombre por el hombre". También contradice el artículo 41: "Todos los ciudadanos tienen los mismos derechos y están sujetos a iguales deberes".

Incumplimiento de tratados internacionales vigentes

He pedido que se cancele la deuda externa de los países menos desarrollados y que se alivie considerablemente la deuda para muchos otros. También me pronuncié a favor de la eliminación del Fondo Monetario Internacional. Es hora de que los países del Tercer Mundo exijan liberarse de un mecanismo que no ha garantizado la estabilidad de la economía mundial... Dije que era necesario otro proceso de Núremberg para condenar el genocidio cometido por el actual orden económico mundial.

Fidel Castro, entrevista Federico Mayor Zaragoza, enero de 2000

Tabla 7. Incumplimiento de tratados y convenciones internacionales en materia laboral.

Organización/ Tratado o Convención	Violación del mandato
CO29 – Convenio sobre trabajo forzado, 1930 (No. 29), y C105 – Convenio sobre Abolición del trabajo forzado, 1957 (No. 105). ILO C029 y C105.	Cuba ha usado el trabajo forzado y obligatorio enviando trabajadores a campamentos agropecuarios permanentes como medio de coerción política, educación o castigo por expresar opiniones políticas contrarias. Además, las movilizaciones para trabajar en proyectos agropecuarios concretos también son violatorias de dichos Convenios.
CO87 – Convenio sobre Libertad de asociación y organización, 1948 (No. 87)	El artículo 1) g) del Nuevo Código Laboral concede a los trabajadores "el derecho a asociarse voluntariamente y formar sindicatos". En la práctica no se permite.
CO95 – Convenio sobre protección del salario, 1949 (No. 05)	Cuba viola este Convenio que prohíbe que se deduzca del salario para pagar directa o indirectamente a una agencia intermediaria estatal por obtener o mantener un empleo.
CO98 – Convenio sobre el derecho a organizarse y a la negociación colectiva, 1949 (No. 98)	La negociación colectiva no existe en Cuba.

CO111 – Convenio sobre Discriminación en el empleo, 1958 (No. 111)	Al seleccionar a los trabajadores que suministra a las firmas extranjeras, Cuba desobedece el mandato de igualdad de oportunidades y de trato en el empleo.
CO122 – Convenio sobre política de empleo, 1964 (No. 122)	La norma en Cuba es seleccionar a tal trabajador para tal puesto, independientemente de calificaciones o habilidades, y en los traslados no se respeta la voluntad del trabajador.
Declaración universal de derechos humanos (Artículo 23)	No se respetan en Cuba: el derecho al trabajo; la libre elección del empleo; condiciones de trabajo justas y favorables; la protección contra el desempleo; el derecho a igual paga por el mismo trabajo; la remuneración justa y favorable; y el derecho a formar sindicatos y a pertenecer a ellos.

Una Cuba democrática no puede ignorar que un delito público y notorio se ha cometido, y que recompensar a los inversores al concederles una ventaja en el tiempo y el costo de la inversión sería enviar una señal equivocada a los recién llegados.

En este punto, es necesario mencionar que España, Canadá, Italia, Francia, Venezuela y otros países que figuran entre las naciones con mayor número de empresas conjuntas en la Isla, han promulgado leyes para proteger a sus trabajadores de las prácticas ilegales y represivas en sus países, entre ellos las de los inversores extranjeros. Los lectores deben ser conscientes del hecho de que muchos de los cubano-americanos que están considerando invertir en Cuba, que se han hecho ciudadanos de España, son ahora parte de la política de la Unión Europea hacia el régimen cubano, lo que duplica su responsabilidad legal y moral en este asunto.

Los trabajadores cubanos y las organizaciones que les representan han planteado su oposición a este estado de cosas. Cada año, la OIT recibe quejas con respecto a los abusos que el régimen cubano ejerce sobre los trabajadores cubanos. Se han celebrado conferencias -como los del Grupo de Trabajo sobre las Mejores Prácticas de Negocios en Cuba - para poner a la opinión mundial al tanto de estas prácticas desleales.

Desde Cuba, el documental clandestino titulado "Bajo el cielo cubano", contiene acusaciones hechas en 2010 por líderes sindicales independientes en Cuba sobre la explotación de los trabajadores cubanos en general y en los hoteles operados por empresas extranjeras en particular. Las organizaciones laborales independientes han estado luchando por ganar un espacio, pero sus líderes terminan en la cárcel las más de las veces. Una pregunta sigue sin respuesta: ¿Cómo ha funcionado este sistema de inversiones en el pasado y cuáles son las expectativas?

Locuras financieras: parasitismo del mejor

Esta vez es diferente: Ocho siglos de locura financiera escrito por Carmen M. Reinhart y Kenneth S. Rogoff, describe el escenario mundial de los préstamos, empréstitos, quiebra -y recuperación - a través de un laberinto de crisis financiera. Cada vez, los expertos han predicho que "esta vez es diferente". Sin embargo, el análisis de los autores de *Ocho siglos...* presenta evidencia suficiente para negar las predicciones de los expertos.

En el caso de más de 57 años, la Cuba de Castro atestigua el hecho de que todos estos años no han sido diferentes. Mi libro titulado *Locuras agrícolas de Fidel Castro: Absurdo, malgasto y parasitismo*, proclama que esta vez **no** va a ser diferente. Casi seis décadas de fracasos e incumplimientos apoyan esta afirmación.

Fidel Castro no ha inventado ninguna nueva técnica de gestión para financiar cientos de proyectos agrícolas, que ya han desaparecido del paisaje cubano. Desde su llegada al poder en 1959, Castro ha tenido financiación gratuita a su disposición:

- Primera fuente (1959-1960): activos sustraídos por la dictadura de Batista: más de $ 25 mil millones.

- Segunda fuente (1959-1963): La tierra y sus mejoras: 25 millones de acres.

- Tercera fuente (1960): Vivienda urbana: varios miles de millones de dólares.

- Cuarta fuente (1960): Sectores industrial y bancario: La Comisión de Solución de Reclamaciones en el Extranjero enumera $ 1.8 mil millones para ciudadanos de Estados Unidos y $ 6.9 mil millones para los exiliados cubanos.

- Quinta fuente (1961): Posesiones de moneda: de 1.187 millones de pesos en circulación, 724 millones fueron entregados, 424 se asumen fuera del país, y 39 millones se suponen en manos "contrarrevolucionarias".

- Sexta Fuente (1968): Lo que quedaba, un total de 55,636 pequeñas empresas.

- Desgaste natural, una parte importante de la depreciación, comenzó un largo camino de deterioro y de edificios en ruinas debido a la vejez y la falta de reparaciones.

- Entones comenzó el juego: Préstamo → Falta de pago → Condonación → Vuelta a pedir prestado.

- El blanco principal fue la Unión Soviética (1960 - 1990): $ 65 mil millones para el sector civil y $ 13.4 miles de millones de dólares para el militar (1960 - 1985).

- Los países occidentales no escaparon: $ 31,7 miles de millones hasta 2008.

- Un largo período de condonar la deuda y comenzar el ciclo de nuevo ha perdurado hasta el día de hoy.

No, esta vez no va a ser diferente. Va a ser igual.

Resultados y oportunidades

Otra medida destinada a esto es una mayor apertura a la inversión de capital extranjero. ¿Quién habría pensado, Shafick, que nosotros, tan doctrinarios, que luchamos contra la inversión extranjera, un día veríamos la inversión extranjera como una necesidad urgente?

Fidel Castro, discurso de 26 de Julio de 1993[71]

Resultados

Es muy difícil llegar a una conclusión con respecto a cuántas empresas y compañías ya están operando en Cuba. Además de la falta de información en detalle, hay contradicciones entre los informes de las organizaciones internacionales y los economistas interesados . Veamos varias fuentes.

La Conferencia de las Naciones Unidas sobre Comercio y Desarrollo (UNCTAD) estima una inversión extranjera acumulada de sólo US $ 215 millones para el período 1990-2009 (incluyendo $ 97 millones de 2007 a 2009). Las cifras reportadas por el Banco Mundial son casi idénticas: $ 210 millones para el período de 1994 a 2009 (y $ 85 millones en 2010). La Encuesta Coordinada sobre la Inversión Directa del Fondo Monetario Internacional informa de $ 583 millones solo para España (finales de 2010).

El Congreso Norteamericano sobre América Latina (NACLA) rebate estas cifras en un artículo escrito por Richard Feinberg, debido a que " chocan con la magnitud de las actividades de inversión extranjera que son fácilmente visibles en la Isla y registradas en los informes anuales de las empresas internacionales que trabajan en Cuba". Feinberg luego se adentra en un ejercicio complejo con cifras proporcionadas por un consultor anónimo con acceso a los datos oficiales. Él reconoce que la falta de información tiene su origen en la "cultura de secretismo del gobierno cubano".

71 http://www.cuba.cu/gobierno/discursos/1993/esp/f260793e.html.

Oportunidades

La 33ª edición de la Feria Internacional de La Habana (FIHAV) se llevó a cabo del 2 al 8 noviembre de 2015 en EXPOCUBA. Como de costumbre, su principal objetivo fue reunir a las organizaciones de todo el mundo interesados en hacer negocios e invertir en Cuba. El año 2015 tuvo la particularidad de un levantamiento potencial del embargo de EE.UU. que aumentaría la presencia de inversores de ese país en Cuba. El evento atrajo a 4.500 expositores de más de 60 países y alrededor de 150.000 delegados. La FIHAV se ha consolidado como el principal canal para promover los vínculos comerciales de Cuba con el resto del mundo.

Tres eventos importantes tuvieron lugar durante las ceremonias. La última *Guía del Inversor en Cuba* y la *Lista de oportunidades para la inversión extranjera* se pusieron a disposición. La tercera característica importante fue el anuncio realizado por el ministro de Comercio Exterior, Rodrigo Malmierca, de que Cuba estaba buscando $ 8.2 mil millones en inversión extranjera para 326 proyectos. La última cifra incluye 80 proyectos más, pero un valor total de $ 500 millones menos que en 2014. Cuarenta de los 246 proyectos anunciados el año pasado se encuentran en "negociaciones avanzadas" y se han eliminado de la lista de este año.

Tabla 8. Oportunidades de inversión propuestas por el gobierno cubano.

Sector	Ubicación		
	ZED Mariel	Resto del país	Total
Procesamiento de alimentos	5	32	37
Industria azucarera		4	4
Comercio al por mayor		1	1
Biotecnología (medicinas)	13		13
Construcción		6	6
Energía renovable	1	13	14
Industria	6	10	16
Minería		10	10
Petróleo		86	86
Transporte		3	3
Turismo		56	56
TOTAL	25	221	246

Fuente: Lista de oportunidades, Ministerio de Comercio Exterior e Inversión Extranjera, La Habana, 2015.

Como se muestra en la Tabla 8, la nueva lista incluye oportunidades en la salud, el turismo, el transporte, la construcción, la agricultura y la energía renovable. El Ministro Malmierca resumió la posición de Cuba de la siguiente manera: "Bajo ninguna circunstancia, incluso sin embargo, queremos volver a ser dependientes de un solo mercado".

Según el ministro Malmierca, el objetivo es atraer al menos $ 8.2 mil millones en inversión extranjera directa por año. ¿Se puede hacer un cálculo de los resultados con las cifras desfavorables proporcionadas por el régimen cubano?

Las estimaciones de los proyectos con inversión extranjera directa después de la promulgación de la nueva ley de inversión extranjera de 2014 son muy difíciles de saber. El Ministro Malmierca señala que 40 de los 246 proyectos anunciados el año pasado se encuentran en "negociaciones avanzadas" y se han eliminado de la lista de este año. De ellos, 6 están destinados para la Zona Especial de Desarrollo del Mariel. Como es habitual, no dio cifras. Si bien la mayoría de estos proyectos son empresas conjuntas con el Estado cubano, algunos fueron financiados con capital extranjero al 100 por ciento.

Caribbean News Now hizo pública la aprobación de un Proyecto Unilever valorado en más de $ 35 millones para una empresa conjunta cubano - holandesa que producirá productos de higiene. Este proyecto amplía la lista de proyectos aprobados en la ZEDM a 11.

La realidad

Obviamente, incluso con la falta de datos fiables, Cuba no pudo alcanzar su meta de $ 2.5 miles de millones del año pasado. ¿Qué hay de este año? El resultado predicho parece pequeño cuando se compara con otros países de la subregión del Caribe. La edición más reciente del informe de la CEPAL señala que después de caer a US $ 6.027 miles de millones de dólares en 2014, la República Dominicana (DR) y Trinidad y Tobago (T & T) son los principales receptores en el Caribe, y absorben el 37% y el 23% de las entradas totales, respectivamente. En el otro extremo, Cuba y Haití reciben sólo pequeñas cantidades de IED, a pesar de sus grandes poblaciones. Es interesante observar que la República Dominicana y Trinidad y Tobago recibieron el 60% de los US $ 6.027 miles de millones de dólares, dejando US $ 2.41 miles de millones (aproximadamente la meta a la que apunta Cuba) para el resto de los países de la subregión del Caribe.

Además de los argumentos contenidos en esta sección, sería muy difícil que Cuba alcanzara su objetivo si las proyecciones de *Cuba Standard* (CS) se hicieran realidad. El Índice de Tendencia Económica Estándar de Cuba (CSETI) sugiere que a partir del cuarto trimestre de 2015 a febrero de 2016, las condiciones de la balanza de pagos para la economía cubana se pusieron más tensas. El Índice de confianza comercial de Cuba (CSBCI) indica que continúa el deterioro de las percepciones y las expectativas para la economía cubana. La puntuación de 57,2 en el primer trimestre de 2016 es el valor más bajo desde que el CS comenzó a medir este índice. En cuanto a las intenciones de invertir en la economía cubana, hay una caída significativa. En el tercer trimestre de 2015, el 45,3 % de los hombres de negocios indicaron un aumento en sus intenciones de invertir en Cuba, mientras que el porcentaje se redujo al 28,8 % en el primer trimestre de 2016.

Un reciente Informe afirma que "Cuba y Haití, que hasta ahora tienen muy pequeñas entradas de IED, primero tendrían que atraer esos flujos con el fin de percibir un impacto positivo significativo". Por cierto, el mismo informe de la CEPAL afirma que Cuba "es la única economía de la región que no reporta datos de IED".

El Ministro de Comercio Exterior, Rodrigo Malmierca, ha reconocido que Cuba necesita una inversión anual de $ 2500 millones de dólares de Estados Unidos para hacer que rebote su economía. No explicó su viabilidad o el procedimiento utilizado para calcular esa cifra. Otro economista cubano proporcionó un escenario más realista.

Juan Triana, exdirector del Centro de la Universidad de La Habana para el Estudio de la Economía Cubana (CEEC), durante un debate público patrocinado por la revista *Temas*, declaró lo siguiente: "Cuba necesita aumentar en casi un 15% su tasa de formación bruta de capital, su tasa de inversión, para ser capaz de lograr posteriormente una tasa bruta promedio anual del 4%. Tardaría 25 años para que este país duplicara su Producto Interno Bruto (PIB). No se necesita un científico ni un médico para calcular eso. Voy a morir y mi hijo va a retirarse antes de que esto se logre. Para entender lo que estamos hablando aquí, dichas altas tasas de crecimiento no son ni una aspiración ni una meta ni un lujo; es la necesidad de este país, si no, vamos a seguir posponiendo el bienestar de las presentes y futuras generaciones".

Un análisis más preciso de una proposición tentadora

La tierra da lo suficiente para satisfacer las necesidades de cada hombre, pero no para su avaricia.

Mahatma Gandhi

A primera vista, los proyectos de inversión parecen ofrecer una oportunidad rentable. Una dosis de precaución es necesaria. La teoría económica básica nos dice que hay un equilibrio entre la incertidumbre y la ganancia, lo cual ha sido demostrado por numerosos estudios económicos. El costo de oportunidad es también una variable importante al considerar la incertidumbre y la ganancia. No sólo existe una relación entre el coste de oportunidad, la incertidumbre y la ganancia, sino que también existe un equilibrio entre ellos. Invertir en Cuba implica un alto grado de incertidumbre debido a su riesgo.

El comportamiento pasado de Cuba parece indicar que la inversión en la Isla no sólo podría resultar un revés financiero grave para las empresas extranjeras, sino además podría terminar con una condena de cárcel para el empresario que se arriesga, como se muestra con los siguientes ejemplos.

- En 1999, Cuba tenía 217 empresas mixtas de Venezuela, España, Canadá e Italia.
- Entre 1999 y 2001, 76 empresas se fueron del país y el número de empresas extranjeras disminuyó a 141.
- En 2002, el gobierno de Cuba reiteró su compromiso con el socialismo y la planificación central y se fueron más empresas. Las que se quedaron en la Isla fueron víctimas de incumplimientos financieros entre 2008 y 2010. La tensión creció entre los gobiernos de España y Cuba a causa del impacto en las empresas españolas.
- La falta de pagos es un hábito crónico en la mayoría de las transacciones de Cuba. La falta de dinero en efectivo disponible ralentiza el proceso, dando lugar a quejas o cierres.
- La probabilidad del cambio en las prioridades de inversión es siempre una amenaza, y las empresas que no están incluidas son hechas a un lado y prácticamente ignoradas.
- En la actualidad, Cuba se encuentra en un proceso de consolidación de la moneda. El desconocimiento de sus planes crea incertidumbre. Las empresas con un cierto grado de

aversión al riesgo deberían esperar al menos hasta que se complete el proceso. (Hasta esta fecha de junio de 2016, no se han realizado cambios conocidos).

- La corrupción rampante en todos los niveles no es un entorno de inversión saludable. El propio Raúl Castro se ha referido en varias ocasiones a que es el peor enemigo de la revolución.
- El Servicio de Inversores de Moody, la famosa firma financiera internacional que clasifica la solvencia de los prestatarios mediante la medición de la pérdida de los inversores esperada en caso de falta de pago, rebajó la calificación del régimen cubano el 23 de abril de 2014. Moody basó su decisión de rebajar la calificación crediticia de Cuba en el aumento del riesgo del colapso económico de Venezuela, un aliado clave cubano. También consideró posibles perturbaciones internas a partir de una transición política desordenada que se traducen en incertidumbre sobre el estado futuro de la economía de Cuba. Sin embargo, el 10 de diciembre de 2015, la misma firma cambió la perspectiva de Cuba de estable a positiva. La decisión se basa en varios factores: a) La dependencia de Venezuela ha disminuido desde 2014; b) El continuo impulso de la reforma y el mayor acercamiento con Estados Unidos han apoyado el desempeño macroeconómico favorable y aumentan la probabilidad de que las sanciones económicas de Estados Unidos podrían seguirse aliviando.

Testimonios de inversionistas anteriores

Nadie aprende por cabeza ajena.

Antiguo proverbio español

Como el gobierno está inmerso en una campaña contra la corrupción, a los inversores extranjeros es probable que se les ofrezcan oportunidades que pueden conducirlos a terminar en la cárcel. Se considera que todas las disputas incumben a las autoridades cubanas. No hay posibilidad de llevarlas a una corte internacional de justicia. He aquí una pequeña muestra:

- Hay que empezar por recordar el primer caso. Era conocido como Jordi, el primer inversor vasco en la famosa discoteca del hotel Comodoro. Cuando las autoridades lo citaron para quejarse de que la discoteca se había convertido en un burdel, Jordi francamente respondió: "Bueno, hasta ahora los santos van a la iglesia y las putas a las discotecas." Le costó $ 4 millones y la expulsión de Cuba.
- El empresario británico Stephen Purvis pasó 15 meses en una prisión cubana.
- El hombre de negocios canadiense Cy Tokmakjian estuvo en la cárcel desde septiembre de 2011, sin ser acusado, hasta hace poco. A finales de abril de 2014, Peter King, un importante miembro del Parlamento canadiense, basado en el caso de su constituyente Cy Tokmakjian, alertó a potenciales inversores de los peligros de hacer negocios con el régimen cubano. El Sr. Tokmakjian está siendo chantajeado. El régimen cubano está solicitando sus activos para liberarlo. El Sr. King declaró que "la comunidad financiera internacional debe pensar dos veces los halagos de los ministros, diplomáticos y funcionarios de comercio cubanos para hacerlos invertir."
- Max Marambio, un chileno que desarrolló un negocio con Fidel Castro, huyó de la Isla cuando fue acusado por el gobierno cubano. Acusó al régimen cubano en una corte francesa para recuperar su negocio expropiado, pero perdió a finales de abril de 2015.
- Sarkis Yacobián, un hombre de negocios canadiense que se construyó una empresa vendiendo automóviles y equipo industrial en Cuba, fue detenido en 2011 y acusado de espionaje. El Sr. Yacobián pasó dos años en la cárcel antes de ser condenado en un juicio de dos días por corrupción y daños económicos al gobierno. Fue condenado a nueve años

de prisión y una multa de $ 7.5 millones de dólares antes de ser liberado en 2014 después de que todos sus bienes fueran confiscados.

- El empresario francés Michel Villand estableció una cadena de panaderías llamada "Pain de París", posteriormente expropiada por el gobierno cubano. En su libro *Mi socio Fidel*, denuncia que sus socios cubanos le defraudaron al mantener dos juegos de libros, y luego le ofrecieron una suma ridícula por su participación.
- Cuba encarceló a ejecutivos de la firma comercial y de inversiones británica Coral Capital Group Ltd por cargos de fraude no especificados. Ellos fueron encontrados culpables de cargos menores en junio pasado y puestos en libertad por el tiempo cumplido, más de un año después. En lugar de deportar, la nueva ley tiene la intención de encontrar los ejecutivos responsables penalmente.
- Stephen Purvis, un hombre de negocios británico fue detenido en Cuba y acusado de una multitud de cargos. Fue liberado 15 meses después.
- Cuba ha cerrado más empresas mixtas de las que ha abierto desde el inicio de las reformas económicas comenzadas en 2011. En 2013, el grupo de bienes de consumo anglo-holandés "Unilever" puso fin a una empresa conjunta de 15 años después de no poder resolver una disputa con el gobierno sobre quién tendría el paquete de control.
- Varios diplomáticos que pidieron el anonimato han revelado graves acusaciones: "El gobierno comunista a veces deja las propuestas de inversión engavetadas sin explicaciones.... Al final, toda la ley sigue siendo discrecional." "Si una empresa tiene éxito, el gobierno a menudo quiere una participación mayor. Se da la bienvenida a la financiación exterior, pero una vez que un proyecto esté operativo quiere hacerse cargo. Usan a los extranjeros donde mejor les convenga. Los echan a un lado tan pronto su utilidad ha acabado".

Dos consideraciones sobre el futuro

La nueva Ley de Inversión Extranjera reitera el compromiso del régimen cubano a respetar los derechos de propiedad de los inversores. Sin embargo, el artículo 27 de la ley de la Zona especial de Mariel pone de manifiesto la posibilidad de revocar la autorización por las siguientes razones: falta de cumplimiento de obligaciones esenciales; por causas de orden público o seguridad nacional; razones de interés social o bien público; y cualquier otra razón que se exprese claramente en la resolución de la autorización. La ley de inversión extranjera tiene cláusulas similares. Anteriores antecedentes en este sentido hacen que sea difícil de creer en la promesa de no expropiación. Por otra parte, la referencia a la compensación no es lo suficientemente clara y la ley establece que cualquier conflicto debe ser resuelto bajo la tutela de las instituciones cubanas.

Sólo cabría especular acerca de lo que sucederá con estas inversiones cuando el estado de derecho finalmente sea establecido en Cuba. El sistema judicial se verá abrumado de exigencias legales como resultado de más de 57 años de acciones arbitrarias y abusivas. Las empresas extranjeras que han conspirado con el Estado cubano para privar a los trabajadores de sus derechos podrían estar en el banquillo de los acusados. Es de pura justicia que los trabajadores explotados tengan su "oportunidad ante un juez" por lo que les fue robado. Tales reclamaciones tendrán una base legal porque los países que invierten en la Cuba de hoy son firmantes de convenios patrocinados por la Organización Internacional del Trabajo y las Naciones Unidas. Un análisis jurídico de Alberto Luzarraga se publicó en 2001. En esencia, el autor sostiene que la estructura de los documentos firmados por el inversor y el Estado cubano es tal que "son nulas y sin efecto desde el inicio debido al hecho de que son basadas en una causa ilícita, a saber: hacer de la mano de obra cubana un objeto de comercio al por mayor y defraudar al trabajador cubano de la mayor parte de su salario".

Si los cubanoamericanos, ya sea como ciudadanos individuales o corporaciones, toman la decisión de invertir, además del potencial problema legal que pueden enfrentar, van a estar ayudando a la explotación de su propio pueblo. El régimen cubano no dudará en robar su dinero duramente ganado en tierras extranjeras, como lo hizo con sus propiedades en el inicio de la revolución para la cual aún no se ha pagado la indemnización.

La espada de Damocles

¿Qué justificación pueden utilizar los imperialistas para pretender destruir esta obra de progreso, de avance? Y no sólo el progreso y el avance, sino de progreso heroico bajo la "espada de Damocles " de los imperialistas, de avance heroico contra todo su poderío, contra todos sus recursos.

Fidel Castro, discurso de Septiembre 10, 1962

La posibilidad de invertir en el sector no estatal de la economía de Cuba ha aumentado después de la reanudación de las relaciones diplomáticas con Estados Unidos y la visita del Presidente Obama a Cuba. Sin embargo, el Gobierno de Cuba en realidad bloquea al sector privado del beneficio de la inversión o el comercio con los EE.UU. ahora que se hace factible. Dado que no se permitirán las inversiones reales hasta que se levante el embargo, muchos empresarios ya están desarrollando planes de negocios y en busca de financiación. La mayoría de ellos no conocen, o ya han olvidado, lo que se llama "proceso de solución de reclamaciones cubanas". Se refiere a la expropiación por valor de millones de dólares por el régimen de Castro durante los cuatro primeros años de la revolución. Los que viajaron a los Estados Unidos en ese momento registraron sus propiedades con el Programa de reivindicaciones cubanas de la Comisión de Reclamaciones Internacionales de los Estados Unidos. Una lista actual contiene cerca de 7000 reclamaciones correspondientes a igual número de propiedades y a un menor número de propietarios.

La Oficina del Asesor Legal del Departamento de Estado de EE.UU. ha estado solicitando asesoramiento de bufetes de abogados con experiencia en este tema. Hay varias opiniones. El gobierno de EE.UU. encargó a la Facultad de Derecho y a la Cátedra de Ciencias Políticas de la Universidad de Creighton el estudio del tema y presentar un informe. Así lo hicieron y redactaron el "Informe sobre la resolución de las reclamaciones pendientes entre Cuba y los Estados Unidos". Más recientemente, el 17 de febrero de 2016, la Sección del Impuesto sobre la American Bar Association ha respondido a una indagación de la Oficina del asesor jurídico del Departamento de Estado de Estados Unidos expresando su desacuerdo con el informe anterior.

Aunque no se puede predecir la atmósfera del momento de la implementación de este programa, es casi seguro que el proceso de inversión se extenderá y podría haber confusión a partir de este debate. Este asunto es de suma importancia debido a que ya está ocurriendo. La espada de Damocles puede terminar en otras manos. Esperemos que no caiga en las de la bruja de Halloween.

Un final apropiado

Nuestro último pensamiento se refiere a la intervención breve del máximo líder durante la celebración del 7º Congreso del Partido Comunista de Cuba. Haciendo uso de su ahora perenne camisa a cuadros y chaqueta deportiva, balbuceó unas pocas frases antes de volver a su existencia otoñal. Aunque el sistema todavía está por cambiar, la era de su poder absoluto ha terminado. Anunció su próximo 90 cumpleaños y la probabilidad de su cercano final. Después de todo, no es inmortal como todos sospechábamos. Dejará atrás un país sumido en el caos, producto de sus desastrosas políticas sociales y económicas. La tentación es demasiado fuerte: "¡Adiós, Comandante!"

Made in the USA
Monee, IL
04 November 2026

67381286R00060